The

Well-Versed

Family

"The law of his God is in his heart;
his feet do not slip."
Psalm 37:31

The

Well-Versed
Family

raising kids of faith through do-able scripture memory

Caroline Boykin

TATE PUBLISHING & *Enterprises*

TATE PUBLISHING
& Enterprises

Tate Publishing is committed to excellence in the publishing industry. Our staff of highly trained professionals, including editors, graphic designers, and marketing personnel, work together to produce the very finest books available. The company reflects the philosophy established by the founders, based on Psalms 68:11,

"THE LORD GAVE THE WORD AND GREAT WAS THE COMPANY OF THOSE WHO PUBLISHED IT."

This title is also available as a Tate Out Loud product.

If you would like further information, please contact us:
1.888.361.9473 | www.tatepublishing.com
TATE PUBLISHING *& Enterprises*, LLC | 127 E. Trade Center Terrace
Mustang, Oklahoma 73064 USA

Published in the United States of America

ISBN: 978-1-5988676-8-8

08.03.13

To my husband, Lindsay,
who has cheered me on every step of the way.
You are a prince among men.

To my precious daughters, Amy and Leah,
who radiate God's love and shine like stars in
the universe.

For the glory of my heavenly Father.
Psalm 71:17–18

Acknowledgements

How many people stop because so few say, "Go!"? *The Well-Versed Family* would never have made it to print with out the many "Go's" I heard from dear friends who believed in me and the need for this message. Your encouragement kept me moving forward. What you are holding is a product of your love, support, and prayer.

Linda Prince, yours was the first "Go" that put this project in motion. Thank you for seeing something I could not have imagined possible.

Robin Kurylo, my kindred spirit, fellow exile and forever friend. Thank you for Colorado and Omaha!

Polly Wells, you believed in this book from the start and encouraged me to action over every cup of coffee.

Karen and Jay Logeman, our Cincinnati family. Your friendship made an eternal impact! We miss you terribly.

Amy Backscheider, my faithful friend and tireless prayer warrior. This book came to be through your many prayers.

Jim Petersen, thank you for championing this book. It never would have happened with out you.

Glenn McMahan, my early "editor." Thank you for the time you spent pouring over those stacks of notes and clippings.

Gene Getz, my lifelong pastor and model. Your love and support are amazing!

Edwina Patterson, thank you for your encouragement and the nuggets of gold.

Karol Ladd, my precious friend. Thank you for your guidance and faithful prayers. You are a treasure.

Linda Rossi, my dear sister. Thank you for your terrific and timely contribution.

Mom and Dad, thank you for your continual love and encouragement!

Grandpa, this book started on Zane Avenue. Your love for God's Word lives on.

Table of Contents

Foreword

If you're like me, memorizing Scripture is something you'd really like to do with your family. It's certainly something you feel you ought to do, but when you mention Scripture memory to your kids they don't exactly jump up and down with glee and ask "When can we start!?!" So you try to teach a verse or two and then it fizzles out and you forget about memorizing Scripture until you hear another sermon praising its benefits.

I've often thought if only I had a creative tool to help me make Scripture memory more meaningful and fun, I could get with the program and start my family on an amazing journey. You see for me personally, memorizing God's Word has made a huge difference in my life. As a young girl my family attended a church that encouraged all the kids to memorize Bible verses. In fact, I got a sticker by my name on a chart in Sunday school for each verse I memorized. Every year I memorized, *"Jesus wept,"* and *"Pray without ceasing"* for obvious reasons. Yet, God used that experience to initiate a love for His Word in my heart.

During my high school years I began memorizing Bible passages on my own without the motivation of a sticker. Why? Because I began to see the blessing and benefit of God's Word hidden in my heart. I had His Living Word in my thoughts at all times. It kept me from temptation and making some awful mistakes in life. It helped me encourage my friends when they were down and needed to hear God's words of strength. Most importantly having Scripture continually on my mind kept my focus on the God who loves me instead of the circumstances that overwhelmed me.

I'm so very thankful for Caroline Boykin's commitment to help families effectively hold God's Word in their hearts. Caroline and I first met during our college years as we both served as counselors at Pine Cove camp in East Texas. Our hearts were knit together over that summer because of our mutual love for God's Word. I specifically remember sitting outside our cabins one weary and hot afternoon and encouraging one another with II Corinthians 4:17–18, "For our light and momentary troubles are achieving for us an eternal glory that far outweighs them all. So we fix our eyes not on what is seen, but on what is unseen. For what is seen is temporary, but what is unseen is eternal." God's Word strengthened our hearts throughout the rest of our summer at camp as well as the years ahead.

Caroline is blessed with a heart for the Lord and a deep commitment to His Word. God has equipped her with creative gifts and talents as well as wonderful teaching skills. This book, *The Well-Versed Family*, is unique, innovative and doable; three characteristics I love when it comes to any parenting resource, but especially for Scripture memory. Your family will be blessed by this helpful tool! Caroline has provided everything you need, all you need to do is prayerfully put it into action and watch the fruit of God's Word grow in your kid's hearts as well as your own. May God bless each of you as you commit your family to the learning of God's glorious Word!

Karol Ladd

(Best-Selling Author of *The Power of a Positive Mom* and other books for families)

Introduction

"Fix these words of mine in your hearts and minds."
Deuteronomy 11:18

After a full morning of peaceful play, a dispute broke out in "Boykin Barbie Land." Amy and Leah, who just turned five and three a few weeks before, had both laid claim to the Pocahontas Barbie with "the good hair," and I could hear their argument escalating as I came up the stairs to their playroom. Settling them both onto Amy's bed, we all knew what was coming next.

It was about three minutes into my predictable ten-minute lecture on "Harmonious Sibling Interaction" when I realized I'd lost my captive audience. Amy's head had fallen like a lead weight onto her pillow, knowing that Mom's monologue could go on for some time. She was nearly asleep. Leah's glassy brown eyes had stopped blinking as she sat staring off into space just over my shoulder.

My daughters had checked out. And I couldn't blame them. Even I had come to dread the sound of my own voice going on and on and on . . .

Putting my head in my hands, I took a deep breath and silently prayed, "Lord, help me! Help me to know what to say and do. I need wisdom. I need your words." Almost instantly a fitting verse I memorized as a child came to mind:

"A gentle answer turns away wrath,
but a harsh word stirs up anger."
Proverbs 15:1

"O.K. guys. Mom's got an idea. We're going to learn a really helpful Bible verse."

Using a few easy hand motions and taking one line at a time, Amy and Leah could say the whole verse in just a few minutes. We talked about what the words meant and how they could help us from getting into painful arguments. For the next few days we reviewed that simple Proverb, and before long the girls had memorized their first verse of Scripture.

Now a simple arm motion of stirring a big pot, along with the question, "Who's stirring up the (anger) pot?" replaced my usual lengthy speech, allowing God's Word to speak to the moment. My husband and I praised the girls for their gentle words and identified the sad consequences of harsh ones. Time and time again we looked to our memory verse to encourage us all toward more peaceful tones.

It seemed a little too easy—and surprisingly effective. So the next week, we memorized another verse. A week later, another. Asking God for guidance, I carefully chose short Proverbs that were easy to learn and practical for our daily family life.

The results were powerful! My little girls were soaking in the Scriptures like sponges. God's Word was not just speaking *for* me—it was speaking *to* me! With each memorized line I could sense the Lord fanning a flame in my *own* heart.

Before long we realized the need to keep track of the verses we were learning. So with limited artistry, I created a "Boykin Heart Chart" and hung it on our refrigerator. It was a large piece of bright yellow construction paper cut in the shape of a heart, laminated, with small slits that held our homemade Bible verse cards. The words around the edge read:

"For the Lord gives wisdom,
and from his mouth come knowledge and
understanding.
Then you will understand what is right and just and
fair—every good path."
Proverbs 2:6, 9

Months later the chart was nearly filled, and we'd moved into learning longer passages, starting with Psalm 23. Each verse we put to memory bore golden opportunities to share the truths of God with my daughters and apply what we were learning. Amy and Leah were taking hold of the Bible, and my husband and I could see buds of fruit popping out everywhere!

Fueled with a renewed passion, I resolved to stay the course with my daughters—making Scripture memory an intentional, consistent, and fun part of our family's routine.

· · · · · · ·

Now years later, and still knee deep in the process, I am continually grateful for my own "spiritual home-schooling." As a very young child, Scripture memory was both modeled and taught to me. My godly grandparents loved and embrace the Bible, and their hearts were fully engraved with God's Word. Faithfully, they invested themselves in building the Word into my life. While helping me memorize line upon line of foundational truth from the King James, they showed me the beauty of the Scriptures.

The impact was profound and eternal! Those verses they taught me, more than any others I've learned over the years, have turned to bedrock in my mind. Powerfully, the Holy Spirit has used them to establish and strengthen my walk of faith in Christ.

As a mom, I've drawn greatly from my godly heritage as I've taught memory verses to my young daughters. Yet early on, I quickly discovered that times had changed. Information *and* activity overload created unique challenges to fulfilling God's command to "impress them [his Word] on your children."[1] Pressures on my time and energy often derailed my commitment to Scripture memory with my girls.

Searching the Christian bookstores for a useful resource, I found the shelves lined with books and videos on parenting and family subjects, but virtually nothing to help families incorporate Scripture memory into their home life. So I began to ask the Lord for simple and effective ways to write his Word on my daughters' hearts.

God provided beyond what I asked or imagined. Scripture memory became a meaningful (and joyful!) time with my girls. Soon, many of our Christian friends were joining our commitment to memorization with their families. Doors of opportunity opened for me to speak to parents on Scripture memory. Ultimately, many encouraged me, including my husband and daughters, to put this message into print.

· · · · · · ·

So, this book is written for you and your family. You may have one child or a dozen. Your family may be blissfully happy or deeply hurting. Perhaps you're a struggling single parent or an involved grandparent, a third generation believer or just starting your new life in Christ.

Wherever you are, this book hopes to inspire and equip you to pursue the treasures of Scripture memory with your kids! The rarest gems will be yours as you go beyond rote memorization and nurture your child's heart with each verse. My prayer is that

God's living Word will be beautifully etched on your family's hearts and minds, and that you will find great delight in the fruit of your labor.

May your kids be blessed to boldly testify with the Psalmist, *"Your statutes are my heritage forever; they are the joy of my heart."*[2]

Part A

Nurturing a Well-Versed Family

"My mother stored my memory, which was then very retentive, with many valuable pieces, chapters, and portions of Scripture, catechisms, hymns, and poems. When the Lord at length opened my eyes, I found great benefit from the recollections of them."

—John Newton, hymn writer of *Amazing Grace*

What's Down in the Well, Comes Up in the Bucket!

> "Surely you desire truth in the inner parts;
> you teach me wisdom in the inmost place."
>
> Psalm 51:6

Recently, a market research interviewer was stopping people in the grocery store after they picked up their bread. One fellow picked up a loaf of Wonder Bread, and the researcher asked him, "Sir, would you be willing to answer a couple questions about your choice of bread?"

The man responded, "Yes, I'd be happy to."

"Fine," said the interviewer. "The question I'd like to ask you is this: Do you feel that your choice of Wonder Bread has been at all influenced by their advertising program?"

The fellow looked shocked and said, "Of course not. I'm not influenced by that sort of thing at all!"

"Well then," he was asked, "could you tell me just why you did choose Wonder Bread?"

And he replied, "Of course I can. Because it builds strong bodies eight ways."[3]

• • • • • • •

There's just no denying it. Each of us is a "human sponge." Our environment, our culture, subtly seeps into our hearts and minds. How are you as an adult being affected?

I remember a conversation I had a few years ago with another mom at a back-to-school party. Our family had just moved back to Dallas after living in Cincinnati for eleven years. We loved Midwest family life, but were glad to return home to our Texas roots. As I shared about our transition, the mom warned me that if I wasn't careful, the glitz of Big D would draw me in like a bee to honey. I assured her (with silent pride) that we wouldn't be conformists . . . I never did like honey.

Predictably, within a few short weeks I found myself shopping for trendy clothes and searching for a new hairstylist. I guess I spoke too soon.

Today, our families are exposed to more of the world's "stuff" than ever before. The advertising industry spends *6 billion dollars a day* in the United States[4] to influence our behavior. And it works!

Music, television, radio, movies, Internet, magazines, newspapers, billboards, and advertisements (Whew!) combined have created an increasingly massive tidal wave of information (and influence) that is unavoidable, overwhelming, and often dangerous. We're saturated but it just keeps coming. So what exactly are we soaking up?

As Christian parents, it's important that we understand what our culture is peddling. The Bible tells it like it is:

> "Practically everything that goes on in the world—
> wanting your own way, wanting everything for yourself,
> wanting to appear important—has nothing to do with
> the Father. It just isolates you from him."
> 1 John 2:16 Msg

The reality of this verse often hits me right between the eyes when I'm shopping with my daughters. On a recent outing to a mainstream, mid-America-type department store, I came across these messages on popular "conversation" t-shirts for girls:

"Me first"
"It's all about me"
"Can't listen—you're dumb"
"I know how you feel—I just don't care"
"Guess where I'm tattooed"
"Not listening"
"Spoiled rotten—Get what I want when I want it"
"I made your boyfriend look"
"I'm HOT—you're Not!"

Now re-read 1 John 2:16 and see if any of those t-shirt messages correlate with what we're told will isolate us from God.

You see, day after day, the brazen, "in-your-face" bombardment of profanity, violence, pornography, degradation, and greed begs our families to conform to its ungodliness. Our kids are a generation at risk in a world that is determined to turn them away from the Living God.

Looking into the Hearts of our Kids
Try for a moment to look into your child's mind with spiritual X-ray vision. What's in there? It's horrifying to think of what can go into our kids' minds everyday!

Now, take that same spiritual X-ray vision and look into your child's *heart*. Really look. How is the barrage from our godless culture impacting who your child is becoming? Their attitudes? Their actions? Their values? Their faith?

Joe White knows kids—and has some wise insights. Since the

70's, Joe and his wife have run the Kanukuk Kamps, hosting over 20,000 campers (ages seven to eighteen) and 2,000 summer staffers each year. As one of the nation's best-loved youth leaders and dad of four grown children, Joe's experience with kids has led him to conclude:

> "It all adds up to one overarching observation: A child becomes what he thinks about. And he thinks about what he sees and hears. Kids are the way they are because of what they're exposed to, what they fill their minds with.
>
> "The human brain was created to be programmed through the senses. The human body was developed to respond to the information stored in the mind. If a child sees and hears often enough about the pleasure of sexual sin, then that is exactly what you can expect that child to do as soon as he or she is able. One plus one always equals two."[5]

Proverbs warns us, *"Above all else, guard your heart, for it is the wellspring of life."*[6] Too many of our kids are suffering (and suffering deeply!) from polluted "wellsprings." Their poorly guarded hearts and minds have left them defenseless. Kids everywhere are succumbing to the lure of sin that is glorified (and advertised) all around them. Our teens are the richest, most populous, best educated, and most physically fit generation in history[7], but sadly many have lost their spiritual footing. Even our youngest children are showing unhealthy signs of cultural wear and tear.

Asking the Tough Questions
Stop and ask yourself. How passionate are you about guarding

your child's heart and mind? What are you willing to invest in building a strong spiritual foundation for your child? How can we, as Christian families, stand firm against the destabilizing forces that undermine our Biblical values and beliefs? What do we do? What *can* we do?

Nearly 3000 years ago, a similar question was asked *and* answered. Psalm 119: 9, 11 says,

> "How can a young man keep his way pure?
> By living according to your word.
> I have hidden your word in my heart
> that I might not sin against you."

Now, I admit, this may seem a rather simplistic answer to a quite complex question. Our lives are multi-faceted. Raising kids in a spiritual war zone is threatening. There's no "magic bullet" to insure our kids develop into faithful and fruitful followers of Jesus Christ.

But one thing *is* for sure. God's Word is living and active. It's at the crux of our faith and directs our obedience to the Lord. The blessings associated with the Scriptures go far beyond anything else at our disposal. Take a look at *some* of the benefits connected with the Word of God. (New Living Translation)

Comfort—"I meditate on your age-old laws; O Lord, they comfort me." Psalm 119:52

Guidance—"Guide my steps by your word, so I will not be overcome by any evil." Psalm 119:133

Wise counsel—"Your decrees please me; they give me wise advice." Psalm 119:24

Peace and Stability—"Those who love your law have great peace and do not stumble." Psalm 119:165

Joy in stressful circumstances—"As pressure and stress bear down on me, I find joy in your commands." Psalm 119:143

Hope—"Do not snatch your word of truth from me, for my only hope is in your laws." Psalm 119:43

Freedom—"I will walk in freedom, for I have devoted myself to your commandments." Psalm 119:45

Prosperity—"But they delight in doing everything the Lord wants; day and night they think about his law. They are like trees planted along the riverbank, bearing fruit each season without fail. Their leaves never wither, and in all they do, they prosper." Psalm 1:2–3

True riches—"Your law is more valuable to me than millions in gold and silver!" Psalm 119:72

Joy and health— "I will never forget your commandments, for you have used them to restore my joy and health." Psalm 119:93

Wisdom—"Your commands make me wiser than my enemies, for your commands are my constant guide. Yes, I have more insight than my teachers, for I am always thinking of your decrees. I am even wiser than my elders, for I have kept your commandments." Psalm 119:98–100

Encouragement in times of grief—"I weep with grief; encourage me by your word." Psalm 119:28

Influence—"May all who fear you find in me a cause for joy, for I have put my hope in your word." Psalm 119:74

Effective prayer—"But if you stay joined to me and my words remain in you, you may ask any request you like, and it will be granted!" John 15:7

The blessings on this list represent every parent's dream for themselves and their children. Who wouldn't want a life filled with all that God has offered us through his Word? And just think—if the Word of God offers us all of this, imagine having it in our memories, always ready and on hand for a moment's need.

In contrast, Psalm 119:92 says, "If your law [synonymous for Word] hadn't sustained me with joy, I would have died in my misery." The truth is, apart from God's Word, the blessings and riches of life dry up and blow away.

Five Ways to Know God's Word

God's Word is deep and vast. To know and understand it is a life-long quest. In the Bible, God gives us five specific ways to learn his Word and apply it to our lives. Each of these approaches to Scripture is both *commended* and *commanded* by the Lord. Let's take a brief look:

1. Hear it.

Hearing the Word is easier today than any other time in history. We can hear Bible teaching 24/7 through Christian radio and television networks. Bible teaching churches and Sunday schools, Christian retreats, seminars, and youth groups offer great opportunities for us to hear the Word taught and preached. (Luke 11:28, Hebrews 10:25)

2. Read it.

The Bible is the world's bestseller but not the world's most read book. Reading through the Bible doesn't have to be a daunting task. Half the books of the Bible can be read in ten to forty-five minutes each, and many of them can be read in less than twenty. If read aloud at an understandable pace, you can go from Genesis to Revelation in one year by reading the Bible just twelve minutes a day. Systematically reading through the Bible gives us the full, broad picture of God's Word. (Deuteronomy 17:18–19, 1 Timothy 4:13)

3. Study it.

The Bible isn't a quick, one-time read. The Holy Spirit inspired the Scriptures so that we have to carefully study—to dig deep—in order to find the true knowledge of God. Bible study goes beyond hearing or reading. It's diligently searching the Scriptures to uncover rich truths and godly wisdom. Great study resources line the shelves of Christian bookstores, supporting the strong resurgence toward more in-depth studying of God's Word. (2 Timothy 3:16–17, 2 Timothy 2:15)

4. Meditate on it.

If you've ever obsessed over something then you know how to meditate. Meditating on Scripture is reflecting over and over again on a verse or passage, allowing the Holy Spirit to shed light on its meaning and application. It allows us to think about God's Word as it relates to our own thoughts and actions.

Meditation is closely tied with Scripture memory. The more Scripture we have fixed in our hearts and minds, the more we have at our disposal to meditate on day and night. Scripture memory makes effective meditation on God's Word possible at any time, any place. (Psalm 1:2–3, Joshua 1:8)

5. Memorize it.

Nothing can substitute for consistently *hearing, reading, studying,* and *meditating* on God's Word. Each one of these is a key for our healthy spiritual growth. But according to the Bible, that isn't enough. We need more. We need the Word woven into the fabric of our hearts through memorization.

For the most part, Scripture memory has vanished from our spiritual landscape. It's headed toward becoming a "dinosaur discipline." Yet, I believe our families need the Word locked in our hearts and minds like never before!

True, the widespread access to information today has made using our memory less of a necessity and more of a challenge. For example, The New York Times, covering everything from international news to business and local affairs, contains more information in one edition than a person in the seventeenth century would encounter in a lifetime.[8] Can you imagine? A lifetime of information in one issue of a major newspaper!

As technology and communication have boomed over the decades, we've become much less dependent on *recalling* information, and more reliant on efficient ways to *access* the information we need. But the Bible isn't just more data for us to access or more information for us to manage. Deuteronomy 32:47 explains,

"These are not just idle words for you—they are your life."

The Lord wants us to "let the word of Christ dwell in [us] richly."[9] Throughout the Bible, we're told to memorize God's Word. Phrases such as

> "Lay hold of my words with all your heart"[10],
> "Do not forget my words"[11],
> "Write them on the tablet of your heart"[12],
> "Keep them in your heart and have all of them ready on your lips"[13],

fill the pages of Scripture and are synonymous for what we call Scripture memory. But, however we refer to it, it means having such a firm grasp on the Word that we are able to recall it accurately in a moment's notice.

The Power of Scripture Memory

At Scott Air Force base in Bellville, Illinois, there hangs a sign: "An Untrained Soldier Is Just a Target." It would seem incomprehensible for us, as a nation, to send our troops into battle without proper training, weaponry or defense. We'd be asking for complete annihilation by our enemy.

Earlier we recognized that our families live in a spiritual war zone and the adversary is looking for easy targets. In Ephesians 6, Paul describes our battle against the "devil's schemes." He warns us to put on our full protective armor made up of truth, righteousness, the gospel, faith, and salvation so that we can "stand our ground" in the midst of intense battle.

Paul then urges us to take "the sword of the Spirit, which is the word of God" and pray. The Word of God is our defensive weaponry. Without it we're sitting ducks!

The Lord Jesus gave us the ultimate example of how to defeat our enemies by wielding the memorized Word. Early in his ministry, the Bible tells us that he "was led into the desert by the Spirit to be tempted by the devil. After fasting forty days and forty nights, he was hungry."[14] It was then, when Jesus was most vulnerable, that the devil came and mercilessly tempted him three times in an effort to destroy his work of salvation.

In all three temptations, the way Jesus responded to the devil's attacks was the same. He didn't get into a lengthy theological argument. But he skillfully refuted Satan without hesitation by accurately quoting passages from Deuteronomy. With each of the three temptations, the Lord Jesus answered in the same way—"It is written . . .," "It is also written . . .," and finally, "Go away! For it is written . . ." And the devil left defeated.

Now let's look at the first of Satan's temptations and consider how a 21st century Christian might play this situation out a little differently:

After a forty-day-and-night fast, the devil comes to tempt John Christian at his weakest point by saying, "If you are a child of God, tell these stones to become bread." John Christian responds by taking out his Palm Pilot (downloaded with five different Bible translations, commentaries, and Hebrew dictionary) and does a quick Free Text Search on "temptation to eat." He finds the correct verse in Deuteronomy 8:3, and just as he begins to read it to the devil, his Palm Pilot goes dead.

Or, John Christian's response may go something like this, "You know, I recently heard a great message on being tempted to eat. It was so good I ordered the CD. The pastor made some really terrific points using Scripture, and I took lots of notes. Let me see if I can pinpoint that sermon outline, and I'll get back to you."

Or perhaps Mr. Christian might answer the devil this way, "I did an in-depth Bible study on 'Temptation to Eat' years ago. My memory is a little fuzzy, but I think it said something about 'man not eating bread alone.' Would you like to join me?"

O.K. This scenario is a bit silly, but it's meant to illustrate an important point. We can read, hear, and study the Word, but we still can't afford NOT to be involved in Scripture memory! There is nothing that can substitute for knowing God's Word by heart.

Our families are in a battle. We will be tempted. And we need an arsenal of truth in our hearts and minds so we are equipped to stand firm. Trust me, the Spirit of God will bring those verses to mind when you need them most.

Thousands of believers throughout history would attest to the strength and victory they've found through Scripture memory. Chuck Swindoll, well-loved author and speaker on *Insight for Living* says:

> "I know of no other single practice in the Christian life more rewarding, practically speaking, than memorizing Scripture. That's right. No other single discipline is more useful and rewarding than this. No other single exercise pays greater spiritual dividends! Your *prayer life* will be strengthened. Your *witnessing* will be sharper and much more effective. Your *counseling* will be in demand. Your *attitudes* and *outlook* will begin to change. Your *mind* will become alert and observant. Your *confidence* and *assurance* will be enhanced. Your *faith* will be solidified."[15]

Scripture memory *is* essential to the fruitful life of the believer. But how about our kids? Is Scripture memory really that important for them? Let's hear again from Joe White, our adolescent and teen expert. In his book, *Faith Training*, Joe tells us:

> "Scripture memory is the single-most-effective life-shaping tool in a parent's toolbox!"[16]

Take a moment to read that line over a couple more times and let it soak in. Joe goes on to say,

> "Scripture memory is to the child what the lamp was to Aladdin.
> It's the diamond to the bride.
> It's the bone to the dog.

It's the flag to the nation.
It's the snow to the skier.
It's the key to the lock."[17]

• • • • • • •

Now I understand, for many, the thought of Scripture memory still elicits a g-r-o-a-n. Past attempts were quickly abandoned. It was too difficult, too boring! You're convinced there's a "short" somewhere in your memory circuitry. Even more, the thought of trying to keep your kids' attention long enough to "impress" God's Word can seem like trying to nail Jell-O to the wall!

You can do it! There's hope and help. Later in this book, we'll look at practical ways to make memorization easier and more meaningful for our families—as well as look for opportunities to apply the verses we've learned.

The Foundations of a Well-Versed Family

> "By wisdom a house is built, and through
> understanding it is established;
> through knowledge its rooms are filled
> with rare and beautiful treasures."
> Proverbs 24:3–4

No pursuit is more important than the cultivation of a godly home. The fruit is sweet—and eternal. Raising kids who love the Lord doesn't occur over night. It happens somewhere in the years between diapers and diplomas, with signs of growth popping up at the most unexpected moments. *Patience* and *perseverance* are great words for parents to remember in the unpredictable "child growing" years.

That's exactly what it takes to successfully grow a Chinese bamboo tree. This unique tree requires steady patience from its grower because all it visibly develops in the first four years is a little bulb and a small shoot. Although you've planted a tree, it appears you are growing nothing more than a big weed. Nonetheless, a mighty tree is taking shape because the first four years are devoted to the development of a massive root system. Then, in the fifth year, the Chinese bamboo tree uses that incredible foundation to launch as much as eighty feet of new growth in just one year.[18] The colossal growth spurt of the Chinese bamboo can't be seen or measured until there is a strong foundational root system it can build upon.

• • • • • • •

Our kids are a lot like the Chinese bamboo tree. It's important for us to understand that the seeds of truth we plant today in our child's heart may not sprout for years to come. Each seed will germinate in its own time through the power of the Holy Spirit. Like the Chinese bamboo, Scripture memory with our kids takes patience, perseverance, *and faith*. It's easy to grow weary waiting for signs of healthy spiritual life to shoot up. But don't lose heart.

Early Scripture memory is a powerful root system for hardy spiritual growth. From the time God gave his people the written Word, he intended that it be deeply rooted in their hearts and minds. One of the most familiar (and foundational) passages in all of Scripture is found in Deuteronomy 6:4–9. Here's the setting:

After wandering in the dessert for 40 years, the Israelites were finally going to see their hopes become a reality. The Lord was about to bring them into the land he had promised to their forefathers (Abraham, Isaac, and Jacob). Though the land flowed with milk and honey, it was also filled with horrendous forms of pagan worship and hostile enemies. God's people were about to walk into complete spiritual darkness. No doubt, the Israelites would face pressures to conform to this evil culture and turn away from the living God. Through Moses, the Lord gave his people instructions for keeping their faith intact from generation to generation:

"Love the Lord your God with all your heart
and with all your soul and with all your strength.
These commandments that I give you today are to be upon
your hearts.
Impress them on your children.
Talk about them when you sit at home and when you
walk along the road,
when you lie down and when you get up.
Tie them as symbols on your hands and bind them on
your foreheads.
Write them on the doorframes of your houses and on
your gates."

The word, "*impress*" means to "strongly affect the mind or emotions" or "to fix in the memory."[19] Moses reiterated the Lord's instructions when he told the Israelites to *"fix these words of mine in your hearts and minds."*[20] Here, the word "*fix*" is defined as "setting firmly in the mind, to make permanent."[21]

God's instructions were crystal clear. His Word was to be indelibly written on the hearts and minds of his people (young and old) from generation to generation.

This passage is timeless wisdom. It's God's blueprint for building a household of faith that can withstand the destructive elements of any culture—past, present, and future. For you and I, these six verses in Deuteronomy provide a beautiful framework for today's Christian family.

In the larger context, this passage can be applied more generally to all five ways of knowing God's Word (see Chapter 1). But when we apply these verses to Scripture memory, we discover a solid foundation for sinking deep spiritual roots. In fact, we'll be referring back to this passage for the next few chapters. Let's start by looking at three foundational principles this passage gives us for growing a well-versed family:

1. Cultivate a Wholehearted Love for the Lord

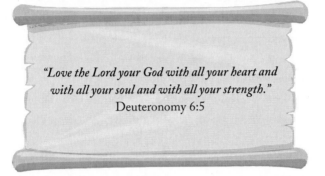

"Love the Lord your God with all your heart and with all your soul and with all your strength."
Deuteronomy 6:5

My kids can read me like a book. They know what I enjoy and what I dread, what makes me happy and what breaks my heart. Their "mom-o-meters" can detect the littlest things without a word being spoken—like my attitudes or emotions, even what moves me to action. They can also keenly discern the sincerity of my faith—whether it's rooted in genuine love for the Lord, driven by duty, or nothing more than a "holy hobby."

As parents, the *best* thing we can do to nurture a well-versed family is to foster our *own* loving relationship with God. Our authentic, personal love for God provides a solid basis for spiritual training in our homes. The Lord wants us to love him with all we have and with all we are, so that we can pass this same love on to our children.

Scripture memory can easily become a project, not a passion. But God wants us to learn his Word as an *extension and demonstration* of our love for him. Jesus said, *"Whoever has my commands and obeys them, his is the one who loves me."*[22] Our love for the Lord is closely linked with his Word. Scripture memory is of little value if we have the words on our lips but they never reach our hearts. In fact, Jesus criticized the Pharisees for their legalism and hypocrisy when he said, *"These people honor me with their lips, but their hearts are far from me."*[23]

Avoiding the Gong

Sitting on a park bench in the cool summer breeze of the Colorado Springs night air, my dear friend Robin and I sat together talking and laughing about everything from varicose veins to memories we shared as Texas transplants to Cincinnati, where we met nearly a decade before. A couple of years had passed since we had seen each other, and our girls' weekend in Colorado provided the perfect setting for a reunion of two kindred spirits.

Since our last time together, God had moved powerfully in Robin's life—leading her into a thriving ministry. She was teaching a weekly Bible study with over 300 women, had written an inspiring book, was a popular speaker at women's events and retreats, and was touching the lives of her neighbors with God's love. In the midst of it all, her marriage embers were still burning strong and her two children were growing into great kids of faith.

Over the evening our conversation turned to "life" and "ministry." In her distinctly southern and genteel voice, Robin shared the poetic words of 1 Corinthians 13, *"If I speak with the tongues of men and of angels, but have not love, I am only a resounding gong or a clanging symbol."*

"Caroline, do you remember seeing the 'Gong Show' on television?"

Of course I did. It was a funny weekly talent show in the '70s where contestants would perform various acts in front of a huge, hanging gong. Often, their performances were so horrible that the celebrity judges would get up from their chairs with a long mallet, walk over to the gong, and give it a big whack. GONG! The loud tone would reverberate, interrupting the performer, and he would be escorted off the stage—disgraced as a loser with no prize money.

"Caroline, a friend of mine recently told me that much of her life had been like the 'Gong Show.' She was in the middle of her 'Christian performance' when her life was 'gonged' for its lack of love."

Robin and I laughed together at the mental picture the story brought to our minds. Then Robin went on, "My ministry can be going gangbusters, but if I'm serving the Lord out of duty or obligation—BAM! The gong will sound. If my ministry is feeding my ego—WHAM! There's that noise again. My ministry means *nothing* if my life is 'gonged' by my heavenly Judge because I didn't have love. I want *everything* I do to be motivated by God's love."

I still chuckle to myself when thinking about how funny our conversation became as we pictured ourselves being "gonged" as wives, mothers, and friends at the most unexpected times.

But what Robin shared really hit home. Anything that we do that is not motivated by the love of God *is* like a gong. How many times had I acted without love, not realizing that even my most noble actions had been given the resounding "GONG"?

You may be asking yourself, what does all this have to do with Scripture memory? Everything! You see, if we can quote the whole Bible from memory, but do it apart from the love of God, we're "gonged." God hears the clanging and our children will be covering their ears before we get to Genesis 1:2.

Likewise, we can teach our kids to memorize volumes of Scripture, but without love it's the annoying sounds of percussion God hears coming from our homes. God doesn't want his children "clanging around." He wants us to be rooted and established in the love he has poured out into our hearts by the Holy Spirit—and embrace his Word with full affection.

2. Lead the Way

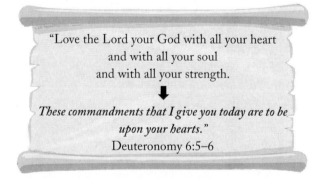

"Love the Lord your God with all your heart
and with all your soul
and with all your strength.

⬇

These commandments that I give you today are to be upon your hearts."
Deuteronomy 6:5–6

A recent cartoon pictured a little boy asking his father a question: "Daddy, what is a Christian?" The father thought for a moment and then replied, "A Christian is a person who loves and obeys God. He loves his friends, his neighbors, and even his enemies. He is kind and gentle and prays a lot. He looks forward to going to heaven and thinks that knowing God is better than anything on this earth. That, son, is a Christian!" The little boy took a couple of moments to contemplate what his father had said, and then asked, "Daddy, have I ever seen a Christian?"[24]

"Lead by example" sounds cliché. But, before God ever instructs us to *"impress"* the Scriptures on our children, he tells us to first put his Word upon *our own* hearts. Modeling Scripture memory prepares the way for our kids to learn.

Personally, the most compelling reason for my early commitment to Scripture memory was the beautiful example my grandparents gave me. Their lives were living proof of the power of

God's memorized Word. Verses flowed effortlessly from their conversations. It seemed they always knew just the right verse for every situation—bringing peace and perspective. Their love for the Lord was reflected in their love for his Word, and it was infectious.

That's the kind of modeling our kids need today. We don't have to be perfect (in fact, we can't be!), but we can come alongside our kids and model a love for learning and knowing God's Word. You can provide a positive example and encouragement by saying things like:

> "I love this passage."
> "These words give me such peace."
> "The Lord brought our memory verse to my mind today when . . ."
> "God is so good to give us that promise."
> "I had a neat chance to share a verse with someone today . . ."
> "Isn't that verse wonderful?"
> "I was just about to ___, when the Lord brought this verse to my mind."

The foundations of Scripture memory are not built by lecture, but by bricks of good example, laid day by day.

Memorize with your kids

The annual speech meet was just a couple of days away and my daughter, Amy, was representing her 2nd grade class by reciting Psalm 23. We were in the car going to a gymnastics lesson with my neighbor, Janie, and her seven-year-old daughter, Lily.

Amy asked if she could say her speech for us. We all agreed

we'd love to hear it and she began, "The Lord is my Shepherd, I shall not want. He maketh me to lie down in green pastures . . ."

As Amy finished, I looked across the seat at my neighbor. Tears were coming down her cheeks. "That was beautiful," she said wiping her tears. "I would love for Lily to learn that Psalm."

I handed Janie the copy of Psalm 23 that I kept in my car for practice during drive time. I explained that I'd formatted the Psalm line by line in a way that made it understandable and easier to memorize. Each verse was printed in a different color and key words were underlined. Janie eagerly took the page and set out to get Lily started memorizing right away.

A couple weeks later in a conversation with Janie, I asked how Psalm 23 was coming along. Janie shook her head in disappointment and said, "Not very well." When I asked her what was wrong, she answered, "I don't know. I gave Lily the copy of Psalm 23. We read through it together and I helped her with all the hard words. I explained that she could learn one line at a time, just as you suggested. And I offered her $15 when she was done. It's been two weeks and she doesn't even know the second verse. I don't know what's wrong! I guess Lily just isn't very good at memorization."

I encouraged Janie to start over and learn Psalm 23 *with* Lily. Perhaps that would make a difference.

Several days later, Lily came through our front door beaming. "Mrs. Boykin, I can say Psalm 23! My mom can't say the whole thing yet. But do you want to hear *me*?"

My dear friend, Janie and I smile about it now, but at the time it had truly not occurred to her to take an active part in helping her first grade daughter memorize the 23rd Psalm, *or* to learn it with her. She thought it was enough to go over the passage, provide some incentive and support, and then let her daughter take it from there.

Children need a faithful partner in the process of memorizing Scripture—someone who will get in there *with* them. If we're working on a new verse or passage, let's enthusiastically come alongside our kids and memorize a line at a time with them. (You'll find they'll definitely memorize more quickly than you and will relish in their ability.)

If our kids are learning a Scripture we already know by memory, let's spur them on each word of the way. Let your family know that when it comes to memorizing the Word, you're all in it together!

3. Recognize, "I am It!"

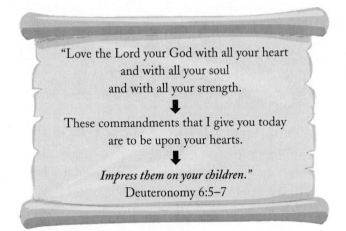

"Love the Lord your God with all your heart
and with all your soul
and with all your strength.

⬇

These commandments that I give you today
are to be upon your hearts.

⬇

Impress them on your children."
Deuteronomy 6:5–7

Not long ago, I had the opportunity to speak to a group of mothers of preschoolers on the subject of Bible memory. After the meeting as I was getting ready to leave, an adorable young mom came up to me and said, "I really liked what you shared about Bible memory today. I didn't realize how important memorizing

Scripture was for my young kids and I like the way you make it fun and interesting. Would it be possible for you to teach my kids to memorize the verses you talked about today?"

When I assured her that she was definitely capable of doing a great job and didn't need my help, she answered politely, "Then, I guess I should go talk to the children's minister at our church and see if they can start something with Bible memory in Sunday school."

This young mom reflects a prevalent and dangerous trend. Parents have become like "general contractors" in the child-building process. We hire various "subcontractors" to do the best job in their area of expertise. Then we oversee, provide support, and keep in touch with how our child is progressing. The general contractor doesn't usually labor with the bricks and mortar. He doesn't even need to own a hammer. He's just making sure the job gets done, and gets done right.

This may work well in education, sports, music and other areas where we need outside expertise. But when it comes to raising spiritually healthy children, the model breaks down.

God, in his wisdom, designed the *family*, and primarily the *parents*, to pass down a godly heritage from generation to generation. In Psalm 78 we read:

> "He decreed statutes for Jacob and established the law in Israel, which he commanded our forefathers to teach their children, so the next generation would know them, even the children yet to be born, and they in turn would tell their children. *Then* they would put their trust in God and would not forget his deeds but would keep his commands."

The most effective way to write the Word on our child's heart isn't accomplished in a formal "institutional" setting. But rather it is through parents who, out of a love and concern for their child, put God and the Scriptures at the center of their home.

Of course, sending our kids to church, youth group, and Christian camp are all *wonderful* ways to build our kids up in the Lord as an *extension* of our training at home. These positive influences are an important part of our kids' Christian experience, especially as they get older. In fact, many of us can testify to the profound impact such ministries have made in our own lives.

But too many parents have delegated a responsibility they can't afford to delegate. Relinquishing our assignment to teach our children to memorize Scripture is unwise. The truth is, many churches have backed away from Bible memory.

According to Darrell Fraley, author and Children and Family Ministry Director, "Scripture memory is all but a lost spiritual discipline in most children's ministries. Unfortunately, this discipline has been connected to a few high expense and labor intensive published programs that are good for Bible memory but difficult to maintain and sustain as a program."[25]

In the context of Scripture memory, Proverbs 22:19 says,

> "So that your trust may be in the Lord,
> I teach you today, even you."

Ask yourself, what am I doing in obedience to God's command to "impress" or "fix" the Word in the hearts and minds of my children, and myself? How intentional am I in rooting my kids in the Scriptures?

Martin Luther King once said, "If not me, then who? If not now, when?" *If we don't fill our children's hearts with the Word, who will?* We can't rely on someone else to encourage our kids toward

Bible memory. And we can't wait for our church or Sunday school to "beef up" their memorization program. There's too much at stake for the next generation.

• • • • • • •

So let's buck the trend and labor with love in building a spiritual heritage for our kids through Bible memory. Cultivating our own wholehearted love for the Lord, memorizing with our kids, and fulfilling our God-given responsibility to impress the Word with love on our children provides a timeless foundation for building a well-versed family of faith!

Making a Good Impression

> "Apply your heart to what I teach,
> for it is pleasing when you keep them in your heart
> and have all of them ready on your lips."
> Proverbs 22:17–18

It's Sunday morning and the Doowell family is scrambling to get out the door. Mindy can't find her shoes. Mom is feverishly trying to lint roll young Kenny's "church pants" which are covered in dog hair from wrestling with Fetch, the family's golden retriever. Baby Nelly needs a last minute, emergency diaper change. And Dad's been sitting in the car for the last five minutes with the motor running.

When, at last, the whole family piles into the car, Dad takes off driving to church at warp speed. In the car, Mom asks Kenny, "Can you say your memory verse for this week, son?"

"Ah, no Mom . . . Um, I don't even know what it *is*."

"Well, Ken, look in your Bible quickly and see if it's written on your Sunday school handout from last week."

"Yeah, Mom, here it is. Sweet. This is a short one! 'Fix these words of mine in your hearts and minds. Deuteronomy 11:18.'"

"Good Kenny. Now just say it over to yourself a few times. You only need one more verse sticker in order to attend the Scripture

Memory Awards next week. I hear they're going to have build-your-own banana splits."

A few minutes later, Kenny goes to his Sunday school class and recites the verse to his teacher (with only three mistakes). He puts a star sticker on the memory chart and later attends the ice cream social.

• • • • • • •

For many of us, this scenario isn't a far-fetched description of what we consider to be Scripture memory. But is this really what God means when he tells us to "*write these commandments that I've given you today on your hearts. Get them inside of you and then get them inside your children*"? (Deuteronomy 6:6–7, Msg)

Clearly, the Lord doesn't want our children to memorize the Word just so they'll get a sticker or an award certificate. God wants our child's *heart* to be *impressed* with his Word. He wants our kids to know his Word as a solid, lifelong foundation for their faith. There's a big difference—a life changing difference!

The childhood years give parents a wonderful, *but fleeting*, opportunity to imprint the Word of God on the moldable, tender hearts of their children. With each passage, the aim is to help our kids gain a sense of comprehension and persuasively bring to bear the truths of God. Rote memorization is not the ultimate goal. The Lord desires that his Word be deeply impressed on our hearts and minds—woven into the very fiber of our being!

Let's look again at our blueprint:

> "Love the Lord your God with all your heart
> and with all your soul
> and with all your strength.
>
> ⬇
>
> These commandments that I give you today are to be
> upon your hearts.
>
> ⬇
>
> *Impress them on your children.*"
> Deuteronomy 6:5–7

Making a lasting impression requires a shift in thinking for many of us from a short term perspective to a long term objective. It also takes time and commitment. Time with our kids. And commitment to memorizing and applying the Word day after day. As we start (or continue on) the process of Scripture memory with our kids, let's look at several practical ways we can help *begin* to effectively impress the Word on the hearts of our children.

Inspire with Incentives

A pastor tells the story of his wife's second grade Sunday school class that was emphasizing Scripture memory. One little seven-year-old, Christian, was beginning to get into the program and was working on his memory verses at home. His dad was inquiring into the whole procedure and asked Christian, "Well, what do you get if you learn these verses? What's the prize or reward?" Christian eyed him with that simple childlike look and said, "We get to learn more!"[26]

Wouldn't it be great if our kids loved God's Word so well that the only motivation they needed to put it to memory was the chance to learn more? O.K., so maybe our kids won't express that kind of enthusiasm for Scripture memory (although you may be surprised!). Good incentives can keep our kids motivated and committed to memorization. While never the *ultimate goal*, giving our kids a worthy return for memorization helps engage them in the process and makes way for a lasting impression on their hearts and minds to be made.

Motivating incentives for our young children are easy to find. Just think about what they like to do, where they like to go, what makes them "light up." Then offer that reward after they can quote a passage word for word and give it's meaning in their own simple way. Some suggestions might be:

- a family picnic in the park

- a favorite meal

- their favorite cake (you could decorate it with the verse reference on top)

- an ice cream outing with a special friend

- bowling, rock climbing, or ice skating

- a fun family movie night at home or seeing a good movie at the theater

- an extra 30 minutes before bedtime

- a "No Chore" pass

- some one-on-one time with mom and dad

- . . . the list could go on.

We've found that our kids were very easy to motivate when they were young. Most of the rewards were things we enjoyed doing as a family anyway, so they weren't adding any extra expense. Keep in mind, the greatest incentive is often positive recognition. Celebrate their accomplishments in Scripture memory. Videotape them quoting a longer passage or chapter. Clap, whistle, cheer! They've just found a piece of hidden treasure that is priceless. Your young kids will beam with accomplishment.

As our children get a little older, added activities and responsibilities squeeze their time. School work, sports, music lessons, youth group, friends, odd jobs for spending money, and needed leisure time can fill every waking moment of our kids' day. Yet, putting the Scriptures to memory is still a wise investment of their time. It's up to us, as parents, to keep our kids inspired and on track with God's Word in their late adolescent and teen years. Consider what Joe White (our *WVF* youth expert) writes about motivating his own teenage kids:

> "I told them that if they would memorize a medium-sized book, God would give them the blessing and I'd give them a chunk of money to spend anyway they chose. I told them that if they'd memorize two medium-sized books (Titus and Philemon–not!) and live by them, I'd give them a car–not a BMW, but a reasonable car that we could afford. (For many of you reading this, even a decent used car is beyond your means. You know what you can and can't afford. But my point is to offer a reward that's sufficiently motivating and commensurate with your child's accomplishment.)

> "The process has been the single most exciting adventure I've ever been on! I'm now on chapter one of book two with my youngest. None of them quit when they finished the goal. Kid number two has

memorized three books to date and has the younger
two memorizing Scripture in her car as she taxis
them to school each day! The passion continues to
spark their own initiative. We've argued, cried, failed,
been through junior-high temptations and high-
school broken dreams like every other family, but
my how the Word of God has been there to guide us!
Folks, it works!"[27]

Take some time and think about what sort of rewards will
work for your family, and do what's right for you. Providing suit-
able incentives for our kids is a key to keeping them motivated
and committed to Scripture memory—a vital *first step* (not the end
goal) in making a lasting impression. As they grow and mature in
their walk of faith, the Lord himself will become their sweetest
reward, and his Word will turn to gold in their hearts!

Engrave with Encouragement

Several years ago, as I was reading through the Proverbs, a verse
jumped off the page at me, *"The wise in heart are called discerning,
and pleasant words promote instruction."*[28] What a contrast these
words were to a funny newspaper comic I read earlier that same
morning. It showed a mom yelling to her misbehaving toddlers
from the laundry room, "I shouldn't have to scream more than
once!!"[29] Was God trying to tell me something?

"Pleasant words promote instruction." Those words have reso-
nated in my mind over and over, especially as I've spent time with
my girls in Scripture memory. It may seem obvious, but how we
communicate as we teach them the truths of God will determine
how receptive our kids will be.

The Bible reminds us to *"encourage one another daily, so that none of you may be hardened by sin's deceitfulness.*"[30] Our kids need our *daily* encouragement. Without it, they are at risk of developing "sclerosis of the heart." And it's difficult to make an impression on a heart that is hardened.

Over the years as I've talked with many parents about Scripture memory, I'm always saddened when I hear one of them share about how they've used the Bible to discipline their children. I've heard moms tell me how they've punished their children by sending them to their room with a verse or passage to learn. Recently a mom told me how she had her child write out a lengthy paper explaining a passage as it related to the child's offense.

These parents may have noble intentions but their approach is unwise. Hitting our kids over the head with the Word will not positively impress it on their heart. It will only serve to embitter them to view the Scriptures as negative and punitive.

So please remember—keep it positive! Learn the Word with laughter and fun. Don't use the Scriptures to punish or discipline, but share the security and comforts of God's truth. Build your kids up with each verse. Boot negativity and criticism out the door. And make each passage a "Spiritual Happy Meal." You'll find your child's heart will be like putty—pliable and receptive.

Memorizing Scripture will have a lasting, *positive* impression on our kids when we intentionally use encouraging and pleasant words to teach them.

Cement with Comprehension

There is no end to uncovering the profound wisdom of the Scriptures. We could spend a lifetime and still find fresh new insights into the truths of God. Each portion of Scripture is much like a well-cut diamond. As we examine it over and over again, contemplating its meaning, light from the Holy Spirit reveals some new brilliant facet.

With each passage your family puts to memory, take some time to talk about what the passage means—but be careful not to go overboard. Pull out one or two key truths in the verse at a time. I've learned (the hard way) that giving my kids *too much* from a passage becomes overwhelming. Keep it short and simple. Children absorb more in smaller portions.

For example, when I was about five-years-old, my grandpa helped me memorize Romans 12:1 (King James Version and all):

> "I beseech you therefore, brethren, by the mercies of God, that ye present your bodies a living sacrifice, holy, acceptable unto God, which is your reasonable service."

That verse was quite a mouthful for a young girl who could barely tie her shoes. Yet I learned it word perfect. One day, as grandpa was helping me memorize the verse, he asked me what it meant. Wide-eyed and speechless, I really didn't have a clue.

Then he explained, "This verse is really important. There's a word in it that I want you to remember. The word is '*reasonable.*' You see, God isn't asking us to do anything that doesn't make sense—anything unreasonable. He loves you and wants the best for you. He demonstrated that by sending his Son to die on the cross for your sins. When we think about what God has done for us, it is only *reasonable* that we give our lives completely to him in return. It only *makes sense* to serve to the Lord. That's what this verse is saying."

Of course this verse says volumes more, but my grandpa was wise not to give me more than I could absorb. SQUISH. Like a handprint in wet cement, a lasting impression was made. Countless times throughout my life Romans 12:1 has come to my mind, reminding me that it's *reasonable* to live for the Lord.

Pulling out a key word or phrase from a passage can help anchor the Scriptures in our minds. Another way to emphasize meaning is to ask three basic questions from the memory verse:

1. What does this verse say about God?
2. What does this verse say about me?
3. What difference does it make?

Let your children share their answers and insights. Give them a chance to think through the verse. As our kids get older, these questions will help them search for meaning and uncover wisdom from the Scriptures on their own.

When my daughters were around age five or six, and just getting the concept of piggy banks, I'd often offer them a dime to say a verse and a quarter to tell me what it meant. (I smile when I think back to some of their explanations.) Rewarding my girls more money for understanding the verse sent a subtle message—the greater value is in grasping the meaning of a verse, not simply in being able to quote it.

Accomplish with Accuracy

I can still picture little Adam in my mind—his smiling face, white-blonde hair, and those blue eyes that twinkled behind his glasses. He was in my daughter's first grade class at a Christian school in Cincinnati. Every Friday morning before chapel, I volunteered to listen to each student in the class recite their weekly Bible memory verse. Seven-year-old Adam was all boy—and precious! I loved to hear him say his verses, though they didn't come easily for him.

This week's verse was short, only eleven words, and I just knew

Adam was going to nail it. He began slowly, "Levipticus nineteen-eweven." Great! Now the verse . . .

"Do not steal," (pause) "do not lie," (pause) "do not *conceive* one another."

I had to bite my lip to keep from laughing. As I explained to Adam that the word was *deceive*, he looked at me and resolutely said, "Mrs. Boykin, Bible memorization is not my sport."

Learning verses accurately, word for word, is so important. There is power and authority in knowing God's Word accurately. One misstated key word or phrase can easily change the true meaning of a verse. An omitted word or phrase can dilute the impact of a passage.

Too many people today are twisting the Word of God to say what they want it to say for their own benefit. In fact, Satan himself misquoted Scripture in an attempt to deceive Jesus. Matthew 4:6 tells us that Satan tempted Jesus by quoting Psalm 91:11. But he quoted the verse only in part, omitted a key phrase, and tried to subtly change its meaning. Jesus didn't fall for it, and Satan was foiled again.

From time to time, try intentionally leaving out or changing a key word or phrase in a passage you're learning with your kids. See if they can catch the mistake. Then talk about how even a word or two can make a huge difference in the verse's meaning. As we help our kids in Scripture memory, paying attention to learning word for word, we can impress them to be on guard for accuracy.

Precede with Prayer

A father was watching his young son try to dislodge a heavy stone. The boy couldn't budge it. "Are you sure you are using all your strength?" the father asked. "Yes, I am," said the exasperated boy.

"No, you are not," the father replied. "You haven't asked me to help you."[31]

Scripture memory can be a real battle! Remember, the Word is the sword of the Spirit—the powerful weapon our enemy fears most. He will go to great lengths to disarm us by derailing our commitment one way or another.

Understand that the Lord never intended for us to accomplish *His* will in *our own* strength. His plan is for us to fully lean on him and rely on the presence and supernatural power of the Holy Spirit. The Lord, himself, wants to furnish our *every need* in accomplishing his will to impress the Word on our child's heart.

So what do you need today? Is your tension running high and patience running low? Seek his endless resource for calm endurance. Are you lacking wisdom as a parent? God promises he will provide it generously if we confidently ask him.[32] Have you become discouraged as a mom or dad? The Bible says that God can give us joy and peace to restore our hope.[33] Maybe you even lack the will for Scripture memory—God can give you that too![34]

A devoted man of prayer, D.L. Moody said, "Behind every work of God you will always find some kneeling form." All of our families are a "work of God" in progress. His mighty hand is desperately needed to build the Word into our families. So let's:

Pray for Opportunities

Golden opportunities to teach our kids God's Word can easily pass us by if we're not looking for them. When we ask him, the Lord will open doors for us to apply or better understand what we are memorizing. Faithfully, God will give us *exactly* the occasions we need for effective teachable moments. I am continually amazed at how God has swung open doors for us to bring his

Word home in our hearts. (We'll look at some of these in the next chapter.)

Pray For God To Help Us Remember His Word

Information overloaded minds, now more than ever, need the Holy Spirit's help to learn and remember the Scriptures. Before setting out to learn a verse, pray that God will enable the words to sink deep into your family's heart. Ask him to bring the passage to mind when you need it. You can set a powerful example for your kids if you often let them see and hear you pray a simple prayer like,

> "Lord, thank you for your living and powerful Word. In this verse, you tell us . . . Help us to learn it well, and let these words sink deep into our hearts. Please bring this passage to our minds when we need it. In Jesus' name, Amen."

Pray for Rain!

As I sit at my computer writing this section, I can hear the rain pouring down outside. My pansies must be thrilled! They've been waiting awhile for a good soaking.

But, this afternoon's rain makes me think of more than just my flowerbeds. It reminds me of the seeds of truth that have been planted in my daughters' hearts. And it prompts me to pray that the Word in their hearts will be well-watered throughout their lives.

Paul wrote to the Corinthians, *"I planted the seeds, Apollos watered it, but God made it grow. For we are God's fellow workers; you are God's field . . ."*[35]

Let's begin to pray *now* that the seeds of truth we plant through Scripture memory will continue to be nourished and grow. Our children will need watering from other strong believers to keep the soil of their hearts moist.

Pray that God will soak the Word into their hearts in order to prevent his precious "fields" from ever getting hardened. Our confidence lies in knowing God's wisdom will determine every drop of rain that falls onto our child's heart, be it a light shower or a heavy thunderstorm. Our rest is in knowing that *God* will make his children grow as only He can!

Keep On Keepin'

William Carey once said of his biographer, "If he gives me credit for being a plodder, he will describe me justly. Anything beyond that will be too much. I can plod. I can persevere in any definite pursuit. To this I owe everything."[36]

Oh, that I might be a plodder too! The definite pursuit of impressing the Word with love on the hearts of my children begs me to keep taking one step after another. Let's plod together. To this we will owe everything.

Seize the Teachable Moment

> "Teach them to your children,
> talking about them when you sit at home
> and when you walk along the road,
> when you lie down and when you get up."
> Deuteronomy 11:19

Time. We all feel the squeeze, don't we? Over the years, one of the most common questions I hear about Bible memory is, "How do you fit memorization into your day? When is the best time to help kids learn memory verses?"

Because each of our families is so unique, there's really no "one size fits all" approach to Scripture memory. We can teach our kids in any posture (my kids have reviewed verses while hanging upside down off the couch)—and at any time day or night. One creative friend of mine taught her preschool son memory verses while pushing him on the playground swings. With his little feet dangling back and forth, she and her young son would say the words in rhythmic time to the out and back movement of the swing. "We love because . . ."—up, up, up—"He first loved us"[37]—and dooown.

Here again, God's timeless blueprint is our guide:

"Love the Lord your God with all your heart
and with all your soul
and with all your strength.

↓

These commandments that I give you today are to be
upon your hearts.

↓

Impress them on your children.

↓

*Talk about them when you sit at home
and when you walk along the road,
when you lie down and when you get up.*"
Deuteronomy 6:5–7

Although we can teach our kids verses anytime . . . anywhere, most families, especially those with younger children, benefit from a comfortable routine. You can make learning verses a regular part of your day like eating breakfast or brushing your teeth. Here are a few suggestions for building Scripture memory into your family life:

Learn Them When You Lie Down

For many families, the best time by far to memorize Scripture is just before their kids go to sleep. Bedtime can be ideal, especially for younger children. How many little kids do you know would refuse a chance to stay up another ten or fifteen minutes before lights out?

Before our girls hit middle school, bedtime worked best. Often, my favorite part of the day was in the evening when I could lie down by my daughters and help them learn a new verse or add another line to a longer passage we were working on. Some of our greatest conversations came out of those times together. Learning verses at bedtime gave us a chance to relax and focus on the Lord and his Word before we went to sleep. My kids still love it when I tickle their backs while saying a familiar Psalm or passage. We did this as a family for years and it worked beautifully.

By consistently learning verses before bedtime, our kids develop a mindset of thinking about God's Word before they go to sleep. One night, our younger daughter Leah was restless and having a hard time falling asleep. Coming down the hall, I overheard Amy suggesting to her, "Just lay in bed and think of all the verses you know. That's what I do." (Personally, I've tried it and it works better than counting sheep!)

Some of you may be thinking, "I'm just too exhausted most nights." True. Many times I've been so dog tired by the end of the day I felt I couldn't do another thing. But I've found that laying down by my kids in the evening and focusing on God's Word is a wonderful way to unwind at the end of a long day. Psalm 119:28 says, *"Strengthen me according to your word."* The Word can give new strength to even the weariest parent.

Try keeping a verse card on your child's nightstand and start by learning one line of Scripture each night. It works like a dream!

Learn Them When You Get Up

My friend, Christie, is a busy young mom with three-and four-year-old boys. Her commitment to teaching her sons to memorize verses at home started early. Already her four-year-old knows several short passages, and her younger son is on his way.

For Christie, the best time to learn verses is at breakfast. In the morning her boys are fresh and alert, ready to start a new day. Bringing memorization into their morning routine sets the course for the day and creates opportunities to talk about what they are learning as the day goes on.

Perhaps "when you get up" is the best time for you and your kids to put a verse to memory. You could start by learning Proverbs 16:24 while eating breakfast, *"Pleasant words are a honeycomb, sweet to the soul and healing to the bones."* Try serving up a bowl of Honeycomb Cereal™ or honey on toast as a fun association for memory. Your kids will eat it up!

Learn Them When You Drive Along the Road
(Or when you sit in traffic)

A mother of four was telling a friend that it may be time to put a limit on her children's outside activities. When her friend asked why, she replied, "The other day someone asked my three-year-old where he lived and he said, 'In my car seat.'"[38]

We do spend a lot of time in our cars these days. Keeping verse cards in the car is an easy way to review and learn new passages. If you have more than one child in the car, encourage them to review verses with each other.

My cousin, Rochelle, uses car time with her 4-year-old daughter to listen to a Scripture memory CD that puts key verses to music. Often, I'll review memory verses when I'm driving by myself to keep up with those my kids have learned more quickly than me.

Using time in the car for memorization is an ideal occasion to drive the Word home in our hearts.

Golden Opportunities

Have you ever forgotten to pick your child up from school? Sometimes our hectic schedules can make us forget or neglect our most important priorities. It happened some years ago with the transportation system in Great Britain. Complaints were mounting over empty buses that were driving past bus stops full of people. After a thorough investigation, the irrational logic was discovered. The bus drivers said they needed to pass up the crowded bus stops so they could stay on schedule.[39]

Once you've put a verse or passage to memory, golden opportunities to talk about it will pop up everywhere. But just like the British bus drivers, our hectic schedules too often cause us to pass them by. The key is to *look for teachable moments with your child,* and then *slow down long enough seize them.*

Teachable moments will put to heart the verses we've already learned. They build the Scriptures into our lives by giving us a context for remembering them and correlating them to our own experiences. God's Word was never intended to be compartmentalized for occasional "sacred" use. The Scriptures come alive only as we *integrate* them into every aspect of our daily lives.

Parents can make God and his Word the natural topic of conversation anywhere and at anytime during the day. That's what our blueprint from Deuteronomy describes. Taking time for spontaneous conversations or creating our own teachable moments will sink biblical truth and principle deep into the hearts of our kids.

Throughout the years, I've been amazed at how many unplanned opportunities we've had to bring home the verses we've learned as a family. Most often, the best chances to review or learn a passage are those that give our kids a chance to "see" the Word in action. Proverbs tells us that Wisdom is shouting to us from every street corner.[40] When we open our eyes to see it, spiritual truth is everywhere. (We'll look more closely at this concept in the next chapter.)

Here are several examples of real-life teachable moments:

Let it Snow!

It was the first big snowfall of the Cincinnati winter and I was driving my oldest daughter to Kindergarten. The thick covering of snow made everything look so clean and beautiful. Even the large dumpsters behind a grocery store we passed along the way were unrecognizable beneath the blanket of crisp white. As we drove, a verse I had learned as a child came to mind:

> "Come now, let us reason together, says the Lord.
> Though your sins are like scarlet, they shall be as white
> as snow; though they are red as crimson, they shall be
> like wool."
> Isaiah 1:18

On the way home from dropping Amy off at school, I decided this would be a great verse to teach my daughters. I wrote the words out on a couple of index cards, put one in my car and another on Amy's nightstand. Within a couple of days both girls had it memorized it word for word.

From then on, whenever the snow would begin to fall, I'd ask the girls if they remembered the "snow verse." We would say the verse together and talk about the sacrifice Jesus made to cover our "ugly dumpster" sins.

"Even a Child . . ."

The second verse we memorized as a family years ago is one that continues to "speak" to us all:

> "Even a child is known by his actions,
> by whether his conduct is pure and right."
> Proverbs 20:11

Teaching my daughters this Proverb went something like this:

"Adults, like Mom and Dad, have to be careful about our conduct, how we behave. Our actions should be pure and right, especially because we are Christians and want to bring honor to God. Someone may not know my name, but they'll know me by how I act or what I do."

"This verse tells us that even children are known by what they do and how they behave, by whether their conduct is good and right. Just think about the kids at school. If you didn't know their names, how would you refer to them (think of actions)? For example: the girl who shares her crayons, the boy who helps the teacher, the girl who laughs at me, the boy who pushes to be first in line, etc . . ."

"If I didn't know your name, I would know you by the way you play peacefully with your friends, or by your helpfulness around the house, or by your willingness to forgive." (Teaching this verse gave me the chance to build my girls up with qualities and actions that they could feel really good about. This isn't the time to address negative behavior or provide correction.)

As time went on, there were many opportunities to encourage my girls with this Proverb. For example, "Leah, if I didn't know your name, I'd call you Thoughtful. Thanks for bringing the cups in from outside!" "Amy, if I didn't know your name, I'd call you Determined. You really worked hard to learn that piano piece." Or I'd say something like, "Hey, I know you! You're the kid that learns those verses so well! God's got a great plan ahead for all that wisdom!"

A few (less harmonious) times, I would simply whisper in their ear, "Even a child," and that was usually enough to convict. If not, I would ask them, "If I didn't know your name right now, how would you be known?" And then I'd let Proverbs 20:11 speak to their hearts.

This verse applied to my husband and me as well. There have definitely been those times when I've had to confess, "I think today Mom would be known as 'Cranky.' I'm sorry, girls."

Brown Grass and Wilted Bouquets

We had just finished memorizing one of my favorite verses:

> "The grass withers and the flowers fall,
> but the word of our God stands forever."
> Isaiah 40:8

My sadly wilted Mother's Day bouquet was about to be thrown in the trash, when it hit me. This fits perfectly with what we just memorized. Setting the bouquet back on the kitchen counter, I asked my daughters if they remembered the verse we just learned about God's Word. After saying the verse together, we took the verse card for Isaiah 40:8 and taped it to the vase of pitifully "fallen" flowers. This was our reminder that God's Word will remain fresh as a daisy for all eternity—but apart from his Word, everything on earth will end up looking (and smelling) just like that rotting bunch of flowers.

Time and time again, we were reminded of our memory verse as flowers would come and go. Great opportunities to recall the timeless truth of Isaiah 40:8 are everywhere—literally behind every (barren) bush. God's Word never withers and never fails. Seasons come and seasons go, but the Word will stand unaltered for eternity—and watch as worldly wisdom wilts.

Star Gazing

"Hey mom, this verse is in a song I have on a CD." Leah was right. The verse was Psalm 36:5:

"Your love, O LORD, reaches to the heavens,
your faithfulness to the skies."

God's love and faithfulness. We'll never fully comprehend it, but we can learn to completely rest in it. Every time we look into the sky we can be reminded of this verse. No matter what the day's forecast—clear blue, cloudy, or gray—God's love and faithfulness toward us is still the same, and it fills the heavens.

Teachable opportunities to contemplate Psalm 36:7 with your kids are limitless. Talk about it when your child studies cloud formations and the atmosphere at school. How about when your kids take a field trip to a planetarium or learn about the solar system? As you watch a space shuttle lift off, ask your kids, "Do you think the astronauts will be able to measure just how far God's love and faithfulness go? What's that verse we learned?"

My girls used to love to take their beach towels out on the front yard, lie on the ground, and look up at the clouds. We'd find shapes of animals and silly objects in the clouds and watch how the wind carried them along in the sky. I was often moved to remind them, "Wow, do you see that verse up there? The Lord's love and faithfulness fill up the skies!"

Amaze 'N Truth

Most opportunities to talk about the verses we've learned are found in our everyday activities and traffic patterns. Other times, teachable moments seem to be more "divinely appointed." This was one of those unique times—a chance to correlate a powerful passage of Scripture to a unique and memorable experience. These are the teachable moments we pray for—and praise God for.

A couple of summers ago, my husband and I took our daughters on vacation to Breckenridge, Colorado. One afternoon, we discovered the "Amaze 'N Maze" on Peak 8, the world's largest human maze. Amy and Leah were given maze "passports" that were stamped with the time they entered the ten-foot-high structure. The object was to go through the maze and find the four punch stations, each one with a different letter—M*A*Z*E. After getting all four punches on their passports, the girls were to find their way to the EXIT, and have their passport stamped with their finish time.

Above one section of the maze was an observation deck. From the deck, my husband and I could see everywhere our girls were going. We could see all the punch stations, and we could see the exit. Signs were posted throughout the maze, which read, "Wrong Way," "Dead end," "Too Bad," etc.

When Amy and Leah entered the maze, my husband and I had a great time watching them from above. Both girls could easily see us and occasionally we would holler down to them, "You're going the wrong way," or "Turn around." Sometimes they could hear us and other times they couldn't (or acted like they couldn't). We cheered when they found a punch station and groaned as they ran into the same dead end over and over again. From time to time, our girls would look up and ask for help, but mostly they were determined to get through it on their own.

Eventually, they each looked to us for some guidance and made it to the exit with all four punches. We were glad to offer the help. Left on their own, we could have been there for hours… even days!

Looking down on my daughters from atop that observation deck, I couldn't help but think of one of my favorite life verses. The girls had just memorized it a couple of months before:

> "Trust in the Lord with all your heart
> and lean not on your own understanding;
> in all your ways acknowledge him,

and he will make your paths straight."
Proverbs 3:5–6

What comforting truth! As our family walked back to the car, I shared how the maze reminded me of Proverbs 3:5–6. Life can be a lot more confusing and difficult than the world's largest human maze. Only the Lord can see every path we need to take because he has the perfect vantage point—and he wrote the map. We can fully trust God to lead us in the right path if we just look to him for guidance. On our own, we will keep running into the same dead ends over again, and never get our "passport to heaven" stamped.

• • • • • • •

One of the greatest blessings from memorizing Scripture is that it takes the Word with us wherever we go. It allows us to talk about God's truth anywhere at anytime. Short, natural conversations can spring up spontaneously, and they don't require a lot of time and energy. In fact, they can be as simple as just a timely sentence or two.

Teachable moments take the verses we've learned and weave them into the fabric of our child's heart. We can't always schedule teachable times but we can seek them out. We must seek them out. Passing up opportunities to talk to our kids about God and his Word is like stepping over dollars to pick up pennies. We're missing the greater riches.

Chances are we will never have more time with our kids than we do today. Research shows that the time we spend with our children decreases with each year after they are in school (including Preschool). Between the ages of ten and fifteen, the amount of time children spend with their families decreases by *half*.[41]

Make the Scriptures come alive for your kids today! Memorize the Word. Then open your eyes to see it all around you. Talk about it every chance you get! Listen to it speak to your families. There is no greater treasure. And no one can steal your investment!

Developing a Mind for Memory

"I will never forget your precepts,
for by them you have preserved my life."
Psalm 119:93

A New York Times article entitled, "A Lost Eloquence," laments the lost "art" of learning poetry and orations by rote memory. The author, a creative writing professor at the University of Southern California, writes:

"Years ago, when I taught in the graduate program in writing at Columbia, the late Russian poet, Joseph Brodsky was also on the faculty. Brodsky famously infuriated the students in his workshop on the first day of class, when he would announce that each student would be expected to memorize several poems (some lengthy) and recite them aloud. The students . . . were outraged at first.

"There was talk among students of refusing to comply with this requirement. Then they began to recite the poems learned by heart in class—and out of class. By the end of the term, students were 'speaking' the poems . . . with dramatic authority and real enjoyment.

Something had happened to change their minds. The poems they'd learned were now in their blood, beating with their hearts."[42]

• • • • • • •

It's very possible you can identify with the initial reaction Brodsky's students had toward memorization. Most people today resist memorization as arduous and boring. Our memory skills are a bit rusty. We haven't been raised on learning the great thoughts and music of the ages as was the tradition in past generations when "ordinary people" could recite verse after verse, passage after passage.

Even so, God's instructions for us to keep his Word in our hearts and impress them on our children remain forever contemporary. Just imagine the profound impact God's Word would have as more and more believers were able to "speak" the Word "with dramatic authority and real enjoyment" and have it "in their blood, beating with their hearts." Wow! Now *that* would be powerful!

Yet perhaps right now you're thinking, "I can't memorize. I've never been any good at it." More than a handful of times I've seen that wincing look on people's faces when Scripture memory is mentioned. At least 95 percent of the people who begin memorizing the Word do it feeling that they have poor memories.[43] You're not alone!

Understanding the basic keys to effective memorization will get you and your family off to a strong start. Your confidence in your ability will grow with each line you learn. Before long, you'll "own" verse after verse.

First, let's look one more time at our well-versed family blueprint:

"Love the Lord your God with all your heart
and with all your soul
and with all your strength.

⬇

These commandments that I give you today are to be
upon your hearts.

⬇

Impress them on your children.

⬇

Talk about them when you sit at home
and when you walk along the road,
when you lie down and when you get up.

✚

*Tie them as symbols on your hands and bind them on
your foreheads.
Write them on the doorframes of your houses and on
your gates.*"

Deuteronomy 6:5–9

In this passage, we understand that the Lord wants us (parents) to love him with all we've got, and fix his Word on our hearts and minds. It's then that we can successfully impress the Word on our children. With the Scriptures in the heart of our home, we can bring the Word into our natural conversations at anytime, any place.

Finally, the Lord continues his instructions by giving us some practical wisdom for helping us *remember* his Word.

As our Creator, God understands how naturally forgetful we are. He knows that we have short memories and a long inclination for spiritual forgetfulness. That's why God tells us to keep the Word with us, and in front of our eyes. We need the constant reminder!

In this chapter, we'll discover simple ways to remember God's Word over time. Understanding the basics of memorization will help us develop a mind for memory. The 3 fundamental elements for successful memorization are:

1. Repetition and Review
2. Association and Connection
3. Application

1. Repetition and Review

Memorization is essentially a process of learning and forgetting, learning and forgetting—with the periods of forgetting growing shorter and shorter until they are nonexistent.[44] The most basic key to successful memorization is repetition and review—going over and over a verse or passage until it's locked in our memory. It takes an extended period of repetition and review for verses to sink deep into our hearts and minds.

When we first started memorizing verses as a family, we created a simple heart-shaped chart that held our handwritten Bible verse cards. We called it the "Boykin Heart Chart." It was taped to the pantry door in our kitchen where we couldn't help but see it several times a day.

As situations arose, we'd often go to our "heart chart" to see if any verses we learned applied. Keeping the verses we learned in a place where we could refer to them daily and be reminded of them over a period of time wove those verses into the fabric of our hearts.

There are lots of great ways to keep memory verses in front of our eyes for review:

Write verses on index cards and keep them in an index box for the car or home.

Keep verse cards near the kitchen table for review at mealtime, or beside the bed.

Take a verse card with you to the gym or when you go out for a walk. (Repeating the words to the rhythm of your steps helps put them to memory)

Tape verse cards to your bathroom mirror or around your computer screen.

Use a verse card as a bookmark and review it when you sit down to read.

You can even put the verse cards or printed passages in a ziplock baggie, wet it, and then stick it on the shower wall to review in the shower (Thanks, Leah, for this idea!)

When learning longer passages, try typing the verses out on the computer. Make several copies and then put them in plastic sleeves. Keep copies handy at home and in the car. Once you've fully memorized the passage, place the printed sheets into a 3-ring Scripture memory binder for your family or for each child. It's a simple idea, but it will help you keep up with what you are learning and provide an organized means for review.

God wants us to remember his Word. He understands that impressing truth is a process that doesn't happen over night. It takes repetition and review to keep Scripture memory in our hearts and minds.

2. Association and Connection

Not long ago, I watched a fascinating segment on a TV news program. The show featured an interview with a 27-year old Administrative Assistant who was the 1999 winner of the US Memoriad Contest—a sort of memorization Olympics. In the interview, the young Assistant explained that she can remember things by making an association or connection for memory—a symbol, a picture, a coding system, whatever makes sense. Her assertion was that she was "just like everybody else. Anybody can do this." (referring to her astonishing feats of memory)

Florida State Psychology Professor, Anders Ericsson, has studied superior memory for years. He claims there is no credible evidence for photographic memory. However, he believes those individuals with strong memory capacity are actually able to quickly *associate* the information they are receiving in their minds and therefore are able to recall it. They've trained their minds to *see* the information in connection with something that is familiar, or makes sense to them.

Ericsson says that with practice *any* individual can improve their memory if they are interested and motivated to do so. For example, some adolescents have no problem remembering scores between different athletic teams, but then have tremendous difficulty remembering even a single date in a history class.

To demonstrate his theory, Dr. Ericsson conducted a revealing memory experiment. A champion chess player was given a few seconds to look at a chess board whose pieces were positioned as they would be in a match. Then the player was given 2 minutes to reproduce the positions of the pieces on an empty board—which he accomplished almost perfectly.

But when the chess player spent the same amount of time looking at the chess board in which the pieces were placed *randomly*, he had trouble remembering the placement of almost any of the pieces. Why? One board had meaning to the chess master, the other did not.

Dr. Ericsson states "Looking for meaning, in any kind of activity, is a very effective way of improving your memory for it."[45] *MEMORY REQUIRES MEANINGFUL CONNECTION.*

WDJD—What Did Jesus Do?

As the quintessential teacher, Jesus consistently made meaningful "associations" to teach truth in a memorable way. By masterfully using metaphors, similes, and parables, Jesus connected spiritual truth with the culture and knowledge of his listeners. His powerful illustrations gave people from every walk of life an "eye" to see and understand his words through the lens of their own experiences—making a lasting impression on their hearts and minds.

For example, when the Lord called his first two disciples (Peter and his brother Andrew) he connected with their livelihood as fisherman in defining his mission when he said, *"Come, follow me and I will make you fishers of men."*[46] The day after Jesus miraculously fed 5,000 people, he explained to the crowd, *"I am the bread of life."*[47] Jesus revealed the truth of who he is by describing himself as *"the light of the world," "the gate," "the good shepherd,"* and *"the true vine"*[48]—linking new knowledge about his identity to something easily grasped by his listeners.

From the mountainside, Christ illustrated the Father's faithful provisions by directing the multitude to *"Look at the birds of the air,"* and *"See how the lilies of the field grow."*[49] He warned that false prophets are like wolves in sheep's clothing and explained that his followers are the *"salt of the earth."*[50]

Take some time reading the red letters in the gospels, observing how frequently Jesus linked spiritual truth with something familiar and easily remembered. By connecting to their common experiences, Jesus brought his words home in the hearts and minds of his listeners.

That's the goal for Scripture memorization. Associating a passage with something that relates to our everyday life make an impression that goes beyond rote memory. Passages we can *see* and *use* in our daily lives will stick!

Seeing the Word Come to Life

It's exciting to look at the world God created and see his Word come alive. Reminders of God's truth are all around us—offering us encouragement, guidance, affection, and warning. Deliberately teaching our kids to see or picture a verse they're learning will help the Word take root.

When you start to look for them, easy and practical connections for Scripture memory are everywhere—the possibilities are endless. Here's an example:

A Sign of New Life:

Symbols are a helpful way to remember God's Word. One of the most beautiful symbols of the believer's new life in Christ is the butterfly. 2 Corinthians 5:17 says,

> "Therefore, if anyone is in Christ, he is a new creation;
> the old has gone, the new has come!"

This wonderful verse can be a lot of fun to learn as a family. The transformation from caterpillar to butterfly is a vivid picture of the new life God offers us through faith in his Son. After putting the words to memory, let your kids draw a butterfly next to the verse in the margin of their Bibles. Talk with your child about the miracle that occurs when a caterpillar changes into a butterfly. Explain that when we put our faith in Jesus, God miraculously changes us into a brand new creation on the inside.

When your child studies butterflies at school, consider putting 2 Corinthians 5:17 to memory at the same time. You may even want to buy a butterfly kit (they are inexpensive and most kids' toy or science stores carry them). Your kids will watch with anticipation as the caterpillars go through several stages before breaking free from their cocoons as a beautiful new creature. Tape a 2 Corinthians 5:17 verse card to the butterfly kit to reinforce the association you're making for memory.

Making Mneumories

We all use mneumonics—from picking a PIN number associated with a birthday to recalling a spelling rule using a jingle ("i" before "e" except after "c"). Mneumonics are devices that help you remember something by linking it with something else.[51] "WWJD?" is a mnemonic way to remember the phrase, "What would Jesus do?"

In Scripture memory, mnemonics can help us recall a verse or a key phrase in a longer passage. Mneumonic connections can be created by looking at a passage and seeing what words or letters stand out or if there are any patterns or repeats. Here's an example:

The "3 H's" for Humility

One of the most beautiful descriptions of Christ's humility is found in Philippians 2:5–11. As our family put this powerful passage to memory years ago, each of us was personally challenged to apply Paul's words in verse 2:5,

> "Your attitude should be the same as that of Christ Jesus."

When we came to verse 8 in the passage, we created a mneumonic connection—the "3 H's"—that summed up the whole passage for us. The verse reads,

> "And being found in appearance as a man, *he humbled himself* and became obedient to death—even death on a cross!"

The "3 H's" became an easy way for us to remember the passage in Philippians about Christ's humility and our need to imitate his attitude. Often we'd ask ourselves, "Are we demonstrating the '3 H's'?" Or, we'd cheer on a humble attitude with, "Wow, what a great example of the '3 H's'—you're awesome!"

Application

Simply stated, we use it or lose it. Application is the golden key to successful Bible memory. In fact, memorization without application is practically worthless.

Theodore Roosevelt said, "I have a horror of words that are not translated into deeds, of speech that does not result in action."[52] Sometimes the hardest thing to do with the Word is apply it to our own lives. But that's also where the greatest joy is found.

I remember one snowy winter night in Cincinnati. My young daughters were sitting on the bar stools in the kitchen having a bedtime snack. While they were eating their cereal, we were reviewing our Philippians 2 memory passage. In the middle of our review, the phone rang. It was my husband who was out of town on a business trip. He was calling to remind me to put the trash out for pick up the next morning.

It was late. I was tired. And the last thing I wanted to do was round up the household trash and drag the big plastic bins out to the curb in the freezing snow. Without hesitation I started in with my complaints, even going as far as to accuse my husband of a "trash conspiracy"—an intentional plan he devised to be gone on Wednesday nights so he didn't have to take out the garbage.

After venting to my husband for several minutes, our conversation ended. As I hung up the phone, I turned to my daughter and asked, "O.K. Leah. Now where were we?" Leah sat there with her elbows on the counter and her head drooping in her hands. Looking up at me sheepishly, she quietly answered, "Do everything without complaining or arguing."[53]

BUSTED! Only the Sovereign Lord of the universe could have timed that phone call so perfectly. I blew it and we all knew it! What a great opportunity for me to confess my bad attitude, apologize, and let them see the Word get me back on track again.

Believe me, there have been countless more times I've had to repeat that process. I've felt deep pangs of regret from blowing it with my kids. But through it all, they've seen that learning verses isn't just a mental exercise. God's Word is a heat-seeking missile that shoots straight to the heart. It is living and active. It convicts and affirms. It humbles and upholds. It speaks. Applying and obeying the Word through the power of the Holy Spirit is the essence of the well-versed family.

Building a Child's Memory

Helping build your child's memory can start early—even before school. If you have young children, you may be surprised at how well they can memorize verses. *Around age three is an ideal time to begin teaching your child Scripture memory.* Even though a young child may not initially understand the meaning of all the words he's able to recite, he will eventually, and his vocabulary will grow in the process.

In addition, some studies indicate that early memorization may be linked to a greater ability to retain and recall information as a child grows older. Children who have been trained to memorize from a young age develop a "mind for memory" that may help them academically in areas that require memorization and organization of thought.[54]

Many kids today have difficulty with focus and retaining information. Cultivating and training a good memory through early Scripture memorization gives children a treasure chest of wisdom *and* expands their minds. Great memories are not born, they are made!

• • • • • • •

Consistent repetition and review, good association and connection, and practical daily application brings the Word home in our hearts. Developing a mind for Scripture memory can start early, but it's *never* too late.

Choosing "Hearty" Seeds

"The seed is the word of God."
Luke 8:11

The poet Coleridge was visited by a man who had a theory about raising children. He stated, "I believe children should be given a free rein to think and act and thus learn at an early age to make their own decisions. This is the only way they can grow into their full potential."

Coleridge made no comment but simply led the man to his garden. "Come see my flower garden," he said. When the opinionated visitor took one look at the overgrown garden he remarked, "Why, that's nothing but a yard full of weeds." The wise poet declared, "It used to be filled with roses, but this year I thought I'd let the garden grow as it willed without tending to it. This is the result."[55]

• • • • • • •

A child's heart is a garden. And like a garden, their hearts will not automatically flourish spiritually. Our kids are in desperate need of a devoted gardener who will give them time, attention, and cultivation. The pliable soil of a child's heart begs for well-chosen seeds of truth skillfully planted and watered with love. If we leave their hearts unattended the junk seeds of the world will take over!

Trust me; nothing will give you more joy as a parent than to see the fruitful harvest from God's well-planted Word. There's nothing more beautiful and fragrant than a blooming garden of Christlikeness . . . filled with the Spirit's fruit of love, joy, peace, patience, kindness, goodness, faithfulness, gentleness and self-control.

You may already have an idea of what you'd like to begin memorizing. Great! This book gives you a variety of pre-printed verse cards so you can get started right away. But as you begin or continue in the process of Scripture memory it may be helpful to keep these six principles in mind:

Choose "Hearty Seeds" That Are Relevant and Timely For Your Family

Each of our families is a one of a kind. We have our own unique strengths and weaknesses, joys and sorrows. We are in different stages of growth and our interests are diverse. As parents, we can shape and mold our home by choosing to learn verses that are pertinent to our individual families. For example:

Does your family need God's guidance? Are we in a period of transition and uncertainty?

> "Trust in the Lord with all your heart
> and lean not on your own understanding;
> in all your ways acknowledge him,
> and he will make your paths straight."
> Proverbs 3:5–6

Are there unkind words flying around the house?

"Reckless words pierce like a sword,
but the tongue of the wise brings healing."
Proverbs 12:18

Is this a time of blessing or victory for your family?

"Every good and perfect gift is from above,
coming down from the Father of the heavenly lights,
who does not change like shifting shadows."
James 1:17

Have the security threats and war stemming from September 11th created fear and anxiety within your home?

"The name of the Lord is a strong tower;
the righteous run to it and are safe."
Proverbs 18:10

or

"When I am afraid,
I will trust in you."
Psalm 56:3

Are you wrestling with lies? Has someone been lied to? Has someone been lied about?

"The Lord detests lying lips,
but he delights in men who are truthful."
Proverbs 12:22
(We call this the Pinocchio verse)

These verses are practical and powerful. In just a sentence or two these truths can encourage, comfort, and guide us. God's Word takes on a fresh relevance when we memorize Scriptures that custom fit our families.

Choose "Hearty Seeds" for Faith and Obedience

Chances are, if you've been a Christian for any length of time, your faith has run into a few roadblocks. In our world of spiritual superhighways to God, it's often difficult to stay on, what Jesus called, "the narrow road that leads to life." If we, and our kids, are going to keep from making dangerous detours, we must have verses for faith and obedience hidden deep within our hearts.

Faith and *obedience* are essentially the two elements of true godliness. In Ecclesiastes 12:13, King Solomon summed up the essence of the Christian life when he wrote,

> "Fear God and keep his commandments,
> for this is the whole duty of man."

The "fear of the Lord" can be defined as an attitude of respect with actions that are right. Our attitude of respect comes from a true knowledge of God and a faith in his eternal power and divine nature. It's vital that our kids' faith be deeply rooted in the character of God, not just in his mere existence. Verses that build our child's understanding of God's character and nature are essential for healthy spiritual life.

According to Solomon, the second "duty" of man is to keep God's commandments. Obedience. It's more than just doing the right thing. It is the truest expression of our love for God. And it's obedience that brings the greatest joy in the believer's life. Our kids need to have seeds of truth in their hearts that will guide their choices and instruct them in Godly living.

In the classic hymn, "Trust and Obey," James H. Sammis aptly wrote:

> When we walk with the Lord
> In the light of His Word,
> What a glory He sheds on our way!
> While we do His good will,
> He abides with us still,
> And with all who will trust and obey.
> Trust and obey,
> For there's no other way
> To be happy in Jesus,
> But to *trust* and *obey*.

The Christian worldview will never be main-stream this side of heaven. But God's memorized Word for faith and obedience has the power to keep us on track!

Choose "Hearty Seeds" for Salvation

Think about it. How did you become a Christian? What role did God's Word have in your own personal salvation? What did the Word of God say that grabbed your heart and led you to place your faith in Jesus Christ as Lord and Savior? 1 Peter 1:23 says:

> "For you have been born again,
> not of perishable seed, but of imperishable,
> through the living and enduring word of God."

God's Word is at the heart of every single believer's salvation! Having key gospel verses locked in our memory anchors our own faith and enables us to better witness to others.

The Bible is filled with verses that tell us how we can be born into God's family and spend eternity with him. To simplify a bit, I've chosen six key gospel verses that are easily memorized in what I call, the "Six For's":

1. "*For* all have sinned and fall short of the glory of God."
   Romans 3:23

2. "*For* the wages of sin is death; but the gift of God is eternal life through Jesus Christ our Lord."
   Romans 6:23

3. "*For* God so loved the world that he gave His one and only Son, that whoever believes in him shall not perish but have eternal life."
   John 3:16

4. "*For* there is one God and one mediator between God and men, the man Christ Jesus."
   1 Timothy 2:5

5. "*For* what I received I passed on to you as of first importance: that Christ died for our sins according to the Scriptures, that he was buried, that he was raised on the third day according to the Scriptures."
   1 Corinthians 15:3–4

6. "*For* it is by grace you have been saved, through faith— and this not from yourselves, it is the gift of God— not by works, so that no one can boast."
   Ephesians 2:8–9

If you're wondering whether teaching your children verses about salvation will make a lasting impression, be encouraged by the example of John Newton. As an eighteenth century preacher, he is probably best known as the author of "Amazing Grace." At the time of his conversion he was a slave trader first mate on a British ship. During a severe storm at sea, he realized his need for God's mercy. Salvation verses his mother had taught him when he was a child flooded his mind at his moment of need, and he was saved.

From the time our children are toddlers, they can learn verses about salvation. If your kids are a bit older, and don't seem receptive to the gospel, don't loose heart . . . and keep on planting the seeds.

Choose "Hearty Seeds" of Wisdom from Proverbs

If there's one thing our world is sorely lacking today, it's wisdom. Wisdom is the ability to see with discernment, to view life as God perceives it. Or described another way, wisdom is the God-given ability to see life with rare objectivity and to handle life with rare stability.[56]

In the very middle (at the heart) of the Bible, God gives us an entire book devoted to timeless wisdom—the book of Proverbs. Proverbs is the book of heavenly wisdom for your family's earthly walk.

Ours may be the first generation in civilized times that has not raised its young children on the Proverbs. From the beginning of recorded history, these concise sayings which describe the benefit of good conduct or the harm of bad have been used to teach children how to behave.[57] The wisdom of the Proverbs was taught in our schools from the earliest beginnings of public education. *McGuffy Readers* dating back to the Colonial days are filled with

Proverbs and other Biblical references. Wisdom was valued and esteemed in generations past—but times have changed.

It may be helpful to understand that Proverbs are not promises, they are *truisms*. According to the Bible, King Solomon wrote over three thousand proverbs which make up a good part of the books of Proverbs and Ecclesiastes. Solomon's wise proverbs are filled with warnings and advice for living under God's design, protection, and blessing.

Proverbs are practical and powerful—and designed to be memorized. Often there is some repetition of a word or sound that helps with memorization. Most of the sayings in the book of Proverbs are four lines long, with a few shorter, and a few longer. They almost always express a contrast and use vivid figurative language (metaphors, similes) to bring truth home in our hearts and minds.

According to the book of Proverbs itself, parents are the key to passing on the wisdom found in its pages. "My son" occurs 15 times in Proverbs chapters 1–9 and 23 times in the 31 chapters of the book. Proverbs 23 says, "My son, if your heart is wise, then my heart will be glad; my inmost being will rejoice when your lips speak what is right."

You may be surprised by how much fun verses from Proverbs can be to learn. There are great ways to "see" them—associate them—in our daily family life. And, through the power of the Holy Spirit, they really go to work shaping our actions and attitudes. For that reason I've included a section of verses from the Proverbs in the back of this book. Proverbs are "hearty seeds" of pure wisdom for our families!

Choose "Hearty Seeds" for Knowing the Lord Jesus

If someone were to stop you on the street and ask you who Jesus is, what would you say? There has never been a more important question asked in the history of mankind. Each of us, no matter who we are, must one day answer this question—and our response will determine our eternity.

While traveling in Philippi, Jesus privately asked his own disciples, "Who do people say that the Son of Man is?" His disciples answered with a variety of popularly held opinions. Jesus then went on to ask them pointedly, "But what about you? Who do you say I am?" It was then that Peter declared, "You are the Christ, the Son of the living God."[58]

In the gospel of John, the Lord Jesus reveals who he is by describing himself in terms people could understand, but which also have profound meaning as to his claim to be the Christ, the Son of God. These are commonly referred to as the "Seven 'I am's' of Jesus." The Lord Jesus said:

1. "I am the bread of life."
2. "I am the light of the world."
3. "I am the gate."
4. "I am the good shepherd."
5. "I am the resurrection and the life."
6. "I am the way and the truth and the life."
7. "I am the vine; you are the branches."

Each of these "I am" verses is easy to memorize and full of rich truth about who Jesus Christ really is and who he offers to be for each of us personally. (Remember: In the Old Testament, God revealed his name to Moses as—"I AM WHO I AM.")

Teaching your children these seven "I am" verses is like filling their hearts with priceless treasure that will not only equip them to answer who Jesus is for themselves, but to also share the truth of who he is with others. Don't miss this great investment opportunity!

Choose "Hearty Seeds" in Balance

As a degreed nutritionist, the first thing I look for in assessing a healthy diet is balance. That's because a balanced diet is typically nutritionally complete, providing our bodies with all the essential nutrients we need for proper growth.

The Bible is food for our spiritual growth and development, a full buffet of truth. As parents, let's recognize the importance of balance in our children's spiritual diet. It is up to us to evaluate our kid's spiritual consumption and give them the complete, balanced nutrition they need for growing in their faith walk with the Lord.

For example, if we feed our children healthy servings of truth about God's unconditional love but leave out the essential truth about his justice, our children may develop an improper view of God that will ultimately affect their spiritual maturity.

In the same way, if we emphasize verses which are used to correct or reprove behavior but don't give attention to those Scriptures which bring comfort and encouragement, our children may see the Bible in a punitive way that could stunt their spiritual growth.

As we choose "hearty seeds" of truth for our kids to learn, remember to plant a balanced variety from God's Word.

• • • • • • •

Quick Planting Tips:

- Avoid planting (teaching) verses too close together: The seeds of God's Word, like the seeds we plant in our gardens, need room to grow. If we plant them too close they'll likely get choked out. Pace yourself in teaching your kids Scripture memory. Try learning one verse a week. Do a little here and a little there. Take time to talk about what you're learning and let the words really sink in. Spend time reviewing, applying, and "seeing" the Word in your daily home life.

- Too much fertilizer can scorch a plant. If there's one thing I'm guilty of, it's harping on a verse or passage we're learning. Over the years, I've learned (the hard way!) to keep my words short and sweet . . . avoiding the sermons that come so easily for me. Remember that often with our words, less is more. Ask your children questions about the verses you're learning. Let them talk. And be a good listener.

A plant nursery I visited awhile back displayed this sign:

> "The best time to plant a tree was ten years ago.
> The next best time is today."

That's exactly right. And the same is true for planting seeds of truth in the hearts of our children. Today's the day to plant away . . . and in ten, twenty, or thirty years . . .

> "They will be called oaks of righteousness,
> a planting for the Lord,
> for the display of his splendor."
> Isaiah 61:3

The Compelling Case for Scripture Memory

"As the rain and the snow come down from heaven,
and do not return to it without watering the earth
and making it bud and flourish,
so that it yields seed for the sower and bread for the eater,
so is my word that goes out from my mouth:
It will not return to me empty,
but will accomplish what I desire
and achieve the purpose for which I sent it."

Isaiah 55:10–11

In his book, *'Til Armageddon*, Billy Graham writes, "Like Joseph storing up grain during the years of plenty to be used during the years of famine that lay ahead, may we store up the truths of God's Word in our hearts as much as possible, so that we are prepared for whatever suffering we are called upon to endure."[59]

The truth is, none of us knows anything beyond this very moment. The future is held in God's hands alone and he calls us to a walk of faith and not sight. In many ways, investing time and energy in Scripture memory for ourselves and our kids requires active (but not blind) faith.

It's likely that teaching our kids to know and trust God's Word will require some shifting in our priorities. Is it worth it? You could take my word for it, but I want to give you the chance to hear from other voices than my own. So, soak up their words. Hear their personal stories. And let the Holy Spirit light a fire in your spirit to hide the living and active Word in the heart of your home while you have time.

Howard Rutledge at the Hanoi Hilton

When Howard Rutledge's plane was shot down over Vietnam, he parachuted into a little village and was immediately attacked, stripped naked, and imprisoned. For the next several years he endured brutal treatment. His food was little more than a bowl of rotting soup with a glob of pig fat—skin, hair, and all. Rats the size of cats and spiders as big as fists scurried around him. He was frequently cold, alone, and tortured. He was sometimes shackled in excruciating positions and left for days in his own waste with carnivorous insects boring through his oozing sores. How did he keep his sanity?

In his book, *In the Presence of Mine Enemies*, Rutledge gives a powerful testimony as to the importance of Scripture memory. Here is an excerpt :

> "Now the sights and sounds and smells of death were all around me. My hunger for spiritual food soon outdid my hunger for a steak. Now I wanted to know about that part of me that will never die. Now I wanted to talk about God and Christ and the church. But in Heartbreak solitary confinement there was no pastor, no Sunday-school teacher, no Bible, no hymnbook, no community of believers to guide and sustain me. I had completely neglected the spiritual dimension of my life. It took prison to show me how empty life is

without God, and so I had to go back in my memory to those Sunday-school days in Tulsa, Oklahoma. If I couldn't have a Bible and hymnbook, I would try to rebuild them in my mind.

"I tried desperately to recall snatches of Scripture, sermons, gospel choruses from childhood, and hymns we sang in church. Most of my fellow prisoners were struggling like me to rediscover faith, to reconstruct workable value systems. Harry Jenkins lived in a cell nearby during much of my captivity. Often we would use those priceless seconds of communication in a day to help one another recall Scripture verses and stories.

"Everyone knew the Lord's Prayer and the Twenty-third Psalm, but the camp favorite verse that everyone recalled first and quoted most often is found in the Gospel of John, third chapter, sixteenth verse. . . . With Harry's help, I even reconstructed the seventeenth and eighteenth verses.

"How I struggled to recall those Scriptures and hymns! I had spent my first eighteen years in a Southern Baptist Sunday school, and I was amazed at how much I could recall. Regrettably, I had not seen then the importance of memorizing verses from the Bible, or learning gospel songs. Now, when I needed them, it was too late. I never dreamed that I would spend almost seven years (five of them in solitary confinement) in a prison in North Vietnam or that thinking about one memorized verse could have made the whole day bearable.

"One portion of a verse I did remember was, 'Thy word have I hid in my heart.' How often I wished I had really worked to hide God's Word in my heart.

"Remember, we weren't playing games. The enemy knew that the best way to break a man's resistance was to crush his spirit in a lonely cell. In other words, some of our POWs after solitary confinement lay down in a fetal position and died. All this talk of Scripture and hymns may seem boring to some, but it was the way we conquered our enemy and overcame the power of death around us."[60]

Emily's Day

"Sometimes I just get tired of it. Girls in my 6th grade class can be nice one minute and so rude the next. It just gets old . . . and it really hurts. Like last week. I was sitting at lunch with my friends and they started making fun of me for putting my napkin on my lap. OK, so it's a habit. I can't help it that I don't eat like a gorilla. But they kept going on and on and wouldn't stop.

"I was about to blow up at them when I remembered a verse we learned at home. *'A fool shows his annoyance at once, but a prudent man overlooks an insult.'* I decided to not say anything and just keep quiet. If I blew up, it would only make me look bad . . . and they would be gloating for the rest of the day.

"I guess it is good to learn memory verses. They come in handy sometimes when I need them."

Ruth Bell Graham's Collection

"People are writing and talking about 'collectibles.' They can be a hedge against inflation, sort of a cushion in case of depression. They are small items that initially may have cost little or nothing but that increase startlingly in value in a relatively short period of time. Included are old stamps, rare coins, old photographs, paintings, even certain cans and bottles.

"I got to thinking. What would be the best collection for me?

Something that would increase in value; something that would make me really wealthy; something I could share that would be a cushion in case of depression and could provide comfort in case of death of a loved one or in old age.

"I had it! Bible verses. I had started long ago.

"In China, Miss Lucy Fletcher offered us, her students, $5.00 (a lot of money for a missionary's kid) if we would memorize the Sermon on the Mount. Hours and hours of going over and over Matthew 5, 6, 7. When the time came to recite it, I made one mistake so I got only $4.50. But I wouldn't take one thousand times that amount in place of having memorized it."[61]

Linda's Story

"Have you ever read the ending of a book first? Or, have you ever finished reading a book and thought, I wonder what really happens or is this real? Well, this is your chance to read the past, see the present, and predict the future. *Pay attention everyone*!!

"Let's start with a few more details from the past. My younger sister, Caroline, and I are only sixteen months apart in age. In the first and most formative years of our lives, circumstances lead us to spend an enormous amount of our early life and development with our grandma and grandpa. We also had Aunt Lois, who was my bed buddy (she shared her room with me) and Aunt Esther, who was Caroline's bed buddy (she shared her room with her), and then there was Uncle Tom, who wasn't that much older than us. Uncle Tom had the cool fort in the back yard with the 'no girls allowed' sign, but he usually let us in anyway.

"It was a happy time for me. Grandma baked cookies, we learned how to shoot pool in the basement, played Rook, had watermelon seed spitting contests, ran through sprinklers, watched fireworks from the back yard, and played games in the neighborhood with all the other kids, including our best friend, Cindy, who lived right next door. In the winter we made snow angels in the mounds of Minnesota snow, built snowmen and snow forts, and learned how to ice skate at the park down the street where a frozen patch of grass became the rink.

"But like nothing ever is, it wasn't all fun and games. Grandpa and Grandma, in their godly wisdom, decided Caroline and I would memorize 100 verses from the King James Bible. The first verse I remember memorizing was John 3:16. Grandpa would give us the reference, and then gently correct us as we went along saying the verse word by word until we had it perfect and committed to memory.

"So it began. Every few days, Grandpa would add a new verse while we continued to repeat the verses we had already learned. I was always happy when the verse Grandpa chose for the day was a short one like I Thessalonians 5:17, 'Pray without ceasing.' Only then the next day Grandpa would add on I Thessalonians 5:18, 'In everything give thanks; for this is the will of God in Christ Jesus concerning you.'

"I remember one day I just didn't want to learn another verse. It was hard and I wanted to play. Grandpa said, 'Linda, today why don't you count the number of hairs on your head?' I thought, 'O.K., I have this nailed.' Well, of course I couldn't count them, so guess what our verse for that day was? Luke 12:7, 'But even the very hairs of your head are all numbered. Fear not, therefore; ye are of more value than many sparrows.'

"As I looked through the memory verse cards Caroline has provided in this book, many of them are from the 100 verses that our grandparents carefully chose and taught us. Because of their loving dedication and faithful determination, by age nine we had 100 verses tucked away in our hearts.

"On May 31, 2006, my world exploded! Many things had come to light that caused me tremendous hurt, pain, grief, anger, disappointment, depression, fear—you name it. What I really wanted to do was stay in bed and pull the covers over my head. In desperation I prayed, 'God, why is this happening? Help me!'

"Fortunately, I decided that I needed to take action and began working on my 'tool box.' I went to the best internal medicine doctor who gave me medications for the symptoms I was suffering. Our family met with our dear pastor and his wife to facilitate communication and talk about our feelings. My sister, Caroline, recommended a book that I quickly ordered and read. She also invited me to a group meeting that she had been attending for a couple of years. I began seeing a wonderful Christian counselor and even contacted my cousin who sent me homeopathic remedies to try.

"One day, Caroline gave me a bag full of Christian music CD's, each marked with specific songs. My husband put them all together and made copies for everyone in the family. I call the CD, 'Caroline's Compelling Compilation for Recovery.' My wonderful husband and sweet daughter were completely loving and supportive, even though they themselves were suffering. The days went by but it seemed nothing I tried really made anything different or even better.

"Then, one night in total darkness, the short verse, 'Pray without ceasing,' came to my mind like a lighting bolt. I started to pray and thank God for loving me and for his faithfulness. It was then, almost like 'play' was pushed on a tape recorder in my mind, that I started to recall some of the 100 verses I had memorized 40 years ago. I was filled with comfort, peace that truly passed understanding, and hope. Joshua 1:9 came clearly to my mind, 'Have I not commanded thee? Be strong and of good courage; be not afraid, neither be thou dismayed; for the Lord thy God is with thee wherever thou goest.'

"For Christmas in 1970, my grandmother gave me a Bible and inside this is what she wrote:

> To our dear granddaughter, Linda. The Bible says in II Timothy 2:15, "Study to show thyself approved unto God, a workman that needeth not to be ashamed, rightly dividing the Word of truth." We covet for you the best things in life which is to know the Lord Jesus as your Savior and to walk pleasing to Him. With our love, Grandma and Grandpa

"Grandma went to heaven when I was eighteen-years-old and Grandpa will be one-hundred-years-old in November. I've learned many things during my forty-six years, traveled to many places, been given many opportunities, and had financial success. These are not the 'things' my Grandma was talking about. In life, it isn't *if* something tragic or difficult is going to happen, it is *when*!

"My grandparents gave my sister, Caroline, and me a precious gift and an inheritance worth more than gold—100 verses! Whereever you are in your life, single, married, parent, grandparent, daughter, son. . . . .I pray that you will use my sister's book as a tool to imbed God's Word in your heart and the hearts of your children. The future will be filled with hope and inspired by God."

A Final Appeal

Early one morning, before my preschool daughters were awake, my neighbor brought over her two-year-old son for me to babysit for a couple of hours while she ran some errands. As we came into the kitchen she noticed my Bible and a notebook setting open on the kitchen table.

With a sincere expression of concern, she looked at me and

asked, "Is everything O.K. with you guys?" Not really making the connection, I assured her that everything was fine, we were all doing well. "Good," she said. "I saw that you'd been reading your Bible and I thought something might be wrong."

That afternoon we had a sudden, torrential thunderstorm. Looking out at the relentless downpour, I thought about what my neighbor said. I regretted that many times my Bible sat gathering dust on the bookshelf until an unexpected "twister" hit my life. Too often it was the tough times that drove me to God's Word.

In the storms of life, God's children cry out to hear from their heavenly Father through the Scriptures. We know we need the Lord's comfort, wisdom, and perspective. And the Bible delivers!

As the rains continued that day, I was reminded of Jesus' words from Matthew 7—

> "Therefore everyone who hears these words of mine and puts them into practice is like a wise man who built his house on the rock.

> "The rain came down, the streams rose, and the winds blew and beat against that house; yet it did not fall, because it had its foundation on the rock."

When I look back on it now, I realize that my grandparents were facing torrential rains of their own when they were "writing" God's Word on my heart throughout my childhood. As a parent, I am overwhelmed with gratitude for all they invested in teaching me to know and love God's written Word—and to find my life in the Living Word, Jesus. Easily, they could have been knocked down by the strong winds of heartache or drowned by the waters of worry, unable to give me the firm foundation I needed. But they pressed on . . . faithfully taking every opportunity to pour more into my heart and soul.

It's possible you're feeling some rain today. The elements beating against your house may even be overwhelming. Perhaps, as a single parent, you're struggling with the weight of laying a foundation single-handedly. For others, financial crisis has hit home. Illness, divorce, relocation, the loss of someone you love—my heart aches for those who are in the eye of a tornado.

But, don't let your circumstance keep you from giving your children an "eye" to see God's Word in the world around them. Your commitment to Scripture memory won't guarantee to keep your family from getting blown and wet, but it will give you a safe harbor and refuge. Know that it was during one of our greatest storms that I began memorizing verses with my young daughters. The joy that came from learning Scripture together kept me from buckling under the pressures, and left an impression on my children's hearts like a handprint in wet cement.

• • • • • • •

Take a deep breath. Pause. Look around at the spiritual landscape. Think about your kids—what they have and what they need for a lifetime of faith in the Lord. Then think about the generation to follow your children. And the generation after that.

Chances are, if we don't begin the process of memorizing verses with our kids at home now, it will never happen. It just won't. There will never be a better time for planting truth in the hearts of your children than today. In fact, you may not even be here tomorrow.

Discipling your kids through Scripture memory will make an eternal impact on your family and the families of generations to follow. Your time will be well spent. So don't put it off. Today is the best day to grab a note card, choose a verse, and get started.

Part B

Tips and Tools for the Well-Versed Family

Ideas are like rabbits.
You get a couple and learn how to handle them,
and pretty soon you have a dozen.

—Anonymous

Memorable Verse Cards

For years people have used verse cards to successfully learn Scripture memory. They are a tried and true tool for learning verses and you'll find a number of preprinted verse cards in the back of this book. In fact, memory verse cards can become a treasured keepsake for your family . . . especially as your children get older and the truths of those Scriptures take hold in their lives. Here are a few simple ideas for using verse cards for memorization:

Index cards: Write out the verse in short, easy-to-learn lines on a 3X5 or 4X6 index card. Use different colored cards for each Scripture memory category. For example, yellow—Proverbs; blue—Salvation; etc. Or you can use a different color index card for each family member.

When a verse has been applied or served to bring timely comfort, strength or encouragement in your family, write about it on the back of the verse card and date it. This will be a lasting record of the power of God's Word in the life of your home.

Put a small magnetic strip on the back of the verse cards and keep them on the refrigerator for easy reference and review. (Adhesive magnetic strips are available at most craft stores)

Memory Card Box: Keep verse cards in an index card box. You can use card dividers to categorize the verses you've learned. Let your kids decorate the box with paint pens and markers. Keep the box on the kitchen table for review during mealtime or take it in the car for review during longer drive times.

Business Card or Credit Card Holder: Keep *Well-Versed Family* memory verse cards in an inexpensive business card or credit card holder for easy organization, portability, and review.

Make your own memory verses cards using blank business cards. These can be found at office supply stores in a variety of designs.

Scripture Memory Photo Album: Purchase small, inexpensive 4X6 photo albums for each family member. Use 4X6 or 3X5 index cards to write out the memory verses. As you learn a verse, put it in the photo album for review. This will be a wonderful keepsake for your children.

Memory Verse Flash Cards: Let your kids cut out pictures from magazines to make their own associations for remembering the passage you're learning. Paste one or two pictures on the back of the memory verse card. (For example: Proverbs 15:3, "The eyes of the Lord are everywhere, keeping watch on the wicked and the good"—pictures of eyes, eyeglasses, sunglasses) Review the verses by looking at the picture on the index card and then quoting the verse on the other side.

Verse Card Key Chain: Put a hole-punch in the upper left corner of the index verse cards and keep them together with a medal ring holder or key chain.

Basic Bible Memory Tips

Visualize or picture the verse written on the index card.

Repeat the verse over and over again in your mind.

Write the verse several times on a piece of paper.

Emphasize certain words in the verse as you say it over and over.

If you get stuck on a word, don't look at the verse immediately. Work your mind to recall it. This will help impress the word in your mind.

Underline memory verses in your Bible with the same color pencil or pen.

Draw a symbol for associating the verse in the margin of your Bible. For example, draw a heart in the margin next to Mark 12:30, "Love the Lord your God . . ." Draw lips next to Proverbs 12:22, "The Lord detests lying lips . . ."

Take turns letting each family member say the verse and then talk about it. Encourage each child to share their tips for associating/remembering the verse. Give them the opportunity to share how the verse is meaningful to them.

Sing Bible verses to familiar tunes or make up a new melody for a verse you're learning. Let your kids put the verse or passage to a rap beat, and dance to the rhythm. Get silly and have fun while dancing around singing the verse. Psalm 119:54 NLT says, "Your principles have been the music of my life."

Have your kids to take turns acting out a verse or passage you are learning.

Quote a verse incorrectly, omitting or changing a key word. See if someone catches the mistake. Give them a simple reward for knowing the verse accurately.

Write a verse you're learning on the bathroom mirror with a white board or transparency marker.

Review the words to a verse when you exercise—the mind is more alert during and after physical activity.

Team up with other families who are committed to Scripture memory. Share ideas and encouragement. Have a Scripture memory party and give out fun certificates (for "longest passage learned," "most creative recitation," etc). Listen to each other quote memorized passages. Celebrate each family's accomplishments and cheer one another on as you hide the Word in the heart of your homes.

Use memory verses in your prayers. God loves to hear us pray his Word.

Use verse cards as a bookmark to review before and after you sit down to read.

Don't get hung up on references. If learning the verse reference becomes too frustrating and difficult, simplify the process by just learning the book and chapter of the verse.

Changing Bible translations in Scripture memory can be very confusing. If you've already memorized the verse in another version, don't try to change.

Use a timer to review your verses, giving each child the same amount of time (about 3–5 minutes is plenty for younger children).

Refer to the verses you are learning for wisdom in daily situations.

Approach Scripture memory with enthusiasm—as something useful and joyful.

Simple Scripture Memory Tools

Family Verse Art: Choose a key verse or passage as your family's theme or motto. (For example, Proverbs 3:5–6) Have each family member participate in writing the verse/s out on an 8 ½ by 11 or 11 by 14 sheet of construction paper. Decorate the paper as a family, date it, and have each family member sign it. Put it in a frame and hang it in the kitchen or family room. You may consider doing more than one over the years. (This is sure to become a family treasure!)

Let your kids create and decorate an 8 ½ by 11 "verse card" for a new verse or passage you are learning. Put the verse in an inexpensive clear plastic frame. Keep the framed verse on the kitchen counter or on the coffee table in the family room. (In a prominent place like by the TV remote control) Replace or rotate verses with new ones you are learning.

Let your kids create a Scripture memory poster on a piece of poster board. Hang it in their room, the hallway, or family room.

A to Z Bible Collection: Buy each one in the family an inexpensive address book. Write the verses you are learning in the book alphabetically. For example:

C—*Children*—"Children, obey your parents in the Lord, for this is right."(Eph. 6:1)

R—*Rest*—"Rest in the Lord and wait patiently for Him." (Psalm 37:7)

Take these Bible alphabet books with you on family trips and play the Alphabet Verse Game. The first person recites an "A" verse; the next person says a "B" verse, and so on until you've gone through the alphabet.

Bible Sticky Notes: In your child's Bible, put words of encouragement on sticky notes next to the verse or passage you're learning.

Write encouraging memory verses you've learned on sticky notes and put them in your child's school notebook, or on their stereo, alarm clock . . . any creative and unexpected place your child will see it.

Put memory verse sticky notes on your bathroom mirror for review morning and evening.

Memory Verse Flip Pad: Let your child draw his own idea for key words and associations for a memory verse on the front page of the flip pad. Write the verse on the back and keep it handy for review.

Scripture Memory CD: Buy a Scripture memory music CD from your local Christian bookstore or online. Listen to the CD during drive time or at bedtime. (Suggested CD's: *Hide 'Em In Your Heart*, by Steve Green; *Scripture Memory Songs*, by Twin Sisters Productions.)

Scripture Memory Videotape: Record your family reciting verses and longer passages you've learned. Your kids will have fun watching themselves quote the Scriptures they've memorized and the video gives them a lasting memory and a fun way to review.

White Board: Write the verse or passage on a white board. Say the verse. Erase one word and say the verse again. Repeat until the whole verse is erased.

Memory Verse Notes: Write out an encouraging verse you have learned or are working on, and stick it in your child's lunchbox with a note letting them know how much you love and value them. You can put these notes under their pillow, in their drawer, or any other special place they will find them.

Memory Verse Rolodex: Keep a rolodex file of memory cards on your desk and flip to a new verse or passage each day to review before you start your work. Or keep the rolodex of verses on your night stand and flip to a new verse each evening before bed.

Easy Memory Verse Games and Activities

Bible Verse Concentration: Write the words of a memory verse on index cards, one word per card. Make two sets. Shuffle the cards and place them face down. Take turns turning over two cards and matching the words. If you don't make a match, turn the cards face down again, but remember where they are! Continue until you've matched all the words and put the verse together.

Bible Verse Old Maid: Write the words of a memory verse on index cards, one word per card. Make two sets. Add a card with a funny face. Shuffle and deal out all the cards. Choose a card from another player. If they match, lay down the pair. The person stuck with the funny face is the Old Maid. The Old Maid puts the verse cards together in the correct order.

Bible Verse Go Fish: Write the words of a memory verse on index cards, one word per card. Make two sets. Scramble the cards face down. Have each player choose three cards. Take turns asking other players if they have one of the words you have. If a match is made, place the pair on the table. If no match is made, the next player goes fishing. Continue until someone is out of cards, then all the players put the verse cards in the right order.

Sticky Situations: Make up common "sticky situations" your kids are faced with and think about what memory verses might apply. This may be a little tough at first, but it will train our kids to search their memory banks to find practical wisdom and encouragement from the Word.

Finish the Verse: Choose one person in the family to think of a Bible verse you have learned. The one who starts is "it." He or she recites the first phrase of the verse, and then calls the name of another person. Before "it" can count to twenty, the one named must finish the verse. If he or she successfully finishes the verse, he or she gets to start the next verse and call on someone else.

If the person can't finish the verse, he or she loses the turn and "it" may call on someone else and count to twenty again.[62]

Verse Scramble: Write out the verse on index cards—one word on each card. Scramble the cards, then assemble the verse word by word in the correct order. (You could have a contest between family members to see who can put the verse together the fastest.)

Memory Verse Add-On: One person starts by saying the first word of a verse or passage. The next person says the second word, etc. See how far you can get without making any mistakes. (This game also works well with longer passages—letting each person quote one line at a time.)

I Spy . . . A Verse: Look around and find something that can easily be associated with a verse. For example, "I spy a cloud." The family members then try to think of a verse that reminds them of that object. (Answer: "In the beginning God created the heavens and the earth."—Genesis 1:1, or "Your love, O Lord, reaches to the heavens, your faithfulness to the skies."—Psalm 36:7)

Bible reference T-shirts: Once you've memorized a number of passages, let your kids paint the references in lots of bright colors on a white or colored T-shirt using fabric paint. As they wear the shirt, practice reciting the verses by looking at the references.

Fill in the Blanks: Write the verse out with several key words missing and take turns with your child to fill in the blanks.

Sidewalk Chalk: Encourage your kids to have fun writing their memory verse/s on the driveway or sidewalk.

Fun Family "Devo's" for Scripture Memory

Devo One

• • • • • • • • •

"Your word is a lamp to my feet
and a light for my path."
Psalm 119:105

You'll Need:

A puzzle (the fewer the pieces, the better)

A flashlight or lantern (one for each family member, if possible)

A blank index card and Bible for each family member

Activity:

As a family, read Psalm 119:105 and underline it in your Bibles. Encourage your kids to draw a flashlight or light bulb in the margin next to the verse. Then have each family member write the verse out on a blank index card. If your child is too little to write, let them scribble the verse on the card with a crayon or pencil.

Spend a few minutes talking about the verse. Encourage your child's participation by asking them questions about what they think the verse means. Along with their verse card, give each child a flashlight and go to a room that is dark when the lights are turned off. (This is best as a nighttime activity)

With the lights on, lay the puzzle pieces on the floor or a table and begin assembling the puzzle together. After a few minutes, turn the lights off. Ask your kids to keep putting the puzzle together—in the total darkness. Let them fumble around for the pieces and struggle with figuring out where the pieces go. Then ask them to turn on their flashlight or lantern.

Using their flashlight, ask your child to read Psalm 119:105 on their verse card. Give each family member a chance to share what the Psalm means to them now that they are in the darkness. Spend a few minutes memorizing the verse one line at a time. Then have fun finishing the puzzle by flashlight or lamplight.

Share:

In many ways, life is like a puzzle. In the dark, it's impossible to put all the "pieces" of life together so they make sense. Our world is really dark. We need the light of God's Word to show us the best path to take and keep us from harm. This verse tells us that God's Word is our most reliable light source. The Bible shines light on how we can know God, have eternal life, and live in faith and obedience to Him. When we have a problem or question, the Bible gives us the light we need to make good decisions.

Seeing the Word Come to Life:

Opportunities to remember Psalm 119:105 are all around us: when we use a flashlight on a camping path, walk in the protection of a street light, put a nightlight in the hallway, eat a meal by candlelight, or even drive at night with the headlights on. See how many sources of light you can find and then talk about the verse. What would it be like if we didn't have any lights? Or what if we decided never to use any of the lights we have in our house? Would that make sense?

—"Son, remember the night we tried to put the puzzle together in the dark? What was that verse we learned? . . ."

Devo Two
· · · · · · · · ·

"Love the Lord your God
with all your heart
and with all your soul
and with all your mind
and with all your strength."
Mark 12:30

You'll need:

A blank index card and Bible for each family member

Activity:

As a family, read Mark 12:28–30 out loud and underline verse 30 in your Bibles. Let you kids draw a heart shape in the margin next to the verse. Ask: What command did Jesus answer was the "most important one"?

Now, look up Deuteronomy 6:5. Read it together, then underline it and draw a heart shape in the margin next to it. Explain that the book of Deuteronomy is in the Old Testament, written thousands of years before Jesus was born. In the Old Testament, God gave His people this command through Moses. In Mark 12:30, Jesus was quoting Scripture!

Take a few minutes and have each family member write Mark 12:30 on a blank index card in 5 lines (as shown above). If your kids are too little to read and write, let them scribble the verse on the index card. You may want to write each line with a different color pencil or marker to make it easier to remember.

Learn each line together. Starting with the thumb, use one finger for each line and then make a fist for the reference as if to keep the verse tightly in our grasp. Remember . . . this is what the Lord Jesus said was the most important commandment . . . so we want to hang on to it and not let it go.

Notice there are four "with all's." Consider remembering them in groupings of two—heart and soul, mind and strength. Play fill in the blanks with the words until your family can say the verse completely.

Listen to your kids talk about what they think the verse means. Why is this the most important commandment of all?

Now substitute the word "all" with "some of" or "most of." How does this change the way God wants us to love Him? Does God love us? How do we know? (point to the Cross)

Share:

God loves us so much and He wants us to love him too. In fact, the most important thing we can do in our whole life is to love God with all we are—with our affections, with our thoughts, and with our bodies. God wants our love for him to come from the inside out. To love the Lord is to choose to have a relationship with him (like a close friend, or parent) and to follow him by obeying his Word.

Seeing the Word Come to Life:

Make this your Valentine's Day verse. As the February holiday rolls around every year, celebrate your love for the Lord and renew your commitment to love him with all your heart, mind, soul, and strength. Review this verse as you make a Valentine for the Lord

Jesus, or make a holiday placemat with the verse printed on it. Remember Mark 12:30 when you see heart shapes in daily life.

Remind your kids of Mark 12:30 when you see a "strong-man" competition or strength event—connecting it in to loving the Lord with all our strength.

Remember this verse when your kids make a good grade at school—letting them know they are "loving God with their minds" when they apply themselves and work hard in their studies.

Devo Three
• • • • • • • • • •

"For there is one God
and one mediator between God and men,
the man Christ Jesus."
1 Timothy 2:5

You'll need:

A new $20 bill

A blank index card and Bible for each family member

Activity:

As a family, read 1 Timothy 2:5 out loud and underline it in your Bibles. Let your kids draw a cross in the margin. Then have each family member write the verse out on an index card.

Take a moment and explain what the word *mediator* means. (The word *mediator* in this verse means "one who mediates between two parties with a view to producing peace" or a "go-between."[63]) Encourage your kids to talk about the verse. Ask them, how many *Gods* does this verse say there are? How many *mediators* (peace makers) between God and men are there? Who is the mediator?

If you have a staircase, bring your kids over to it and tell them to pretend that the top of the staircase is "heaven" where God lives. (If you don't have a staircase you can use another location—a room, for example—as the pretend "heaven") Show your kids a

new $20 bill and offer to give it to the first child who can find a
way to get up to the top of the stairs . . . under these conditions:

1. They can not touch the stairs, railing, or walls
2. They can not bring anything with them

Give them some time to have fun thinking about how to
accomplish this feat. Dangle the $20 prize as a carrot for their
success in making it to "heaven" at the top of the stairs or the
other room.

When they've exhausted their possibilities, ask them one at a
time to jump on your back and piggy back them to the top of the
stairs (or to the other room).

Share:
You guys tried really hard to make it to the top of the stairs and
win the $20 bill. But it just wasn't possible, was it? The only way
for you to get to the top without using your hands and feet was to
let me carry you. This is what Jesus does for us. On our own, we
can't have peace with God and enter heaven. Our sin keeps us out
of God's presence.

But Jesus is our one-and-only mediator (peace maker) between
us and God. By dying on the cross for our sins, the cross becomes
a bridge to God when we accept Jesus as our Savior. Just like you
kids had to actually get on my back to be carried to the top of the
stairs, so we also have to take action and personally receive the
Lord Jesus into our hearts so that we can have a personal relationship with God and an eternal home with him in heaven.

Seeing the Word Come to Life:
Use the cross as a symbol of Jesus being the one-and-only way
to God in heaven. Remind them of 1 Timothy 2:5 when you see
a cross. From time to time ask them how many *Gods* there are.
How many *mediators*—peace makers—are there between us and

God? Ask them how they know there's only one . . . and then say the verse.

—"Sweetie, climb up on my back and I'll carry you to your room and tuck you into bed. Hey, remember that time you tried so hard to get to the pretend heaven without using your hands and feet? How funny was that! What was that verse we learned? . . ."

Devo Four
. . . .

"Therefore, as God's chosen people,
holy and dearly loved,
clothe yourselves with compassion, kindness,
humility, gentleness and patience."
Colossians 3:12

You'll need:

A coat, a pair of socks, a hat, a pair of gloves, and a pair of pants.

A blank index card and Bible for each family member

Activity:

As a family, read Colossians 3:12 and underline it in your Bibles. Put a clothes symbol in the margin, for example a pair of pants, shirt, or hat. Then have each family member write the verse out on a blank index card.

Spend a few minutes talking about the verse. Ask questions like, what do you think it means when it says we are "God's chosen people"? How does God feel about us? What are we supposed to "wear" as God's children?

Now, let's pretend to put on God's designer spiritual clothes. Lay all the clothing items in the middle of the room. Make the following association for memorizing the verse:

1. Coat—Compassion
2. Socks—Kindness

3. Hat—Humility
4. Gloves—Gentleness
5. Pants—Patience

Have fun putting on each article of spiritual clothing in order. Talk about what each of the pieces of clothes should look like in our actions. Say the verse together line by line until you've learned it together.

Share:
Just as we put on our physical clothes every day, there are "spiritual clothes" God wants us to wear that will identify us as his children. These spiritual clothes aren't the popular "trendy" clothes our culture wears. If fact, God wants us to put on these special spiritual clothes because he loves us and wants us to look like children of the King.

Seeing the Word Come to Life:
Make this your clothes shopping verse! Review the verse when you're in the mall shopping for school clothes or looking for something to wear for a special occasion. Remind your children to think about what they are "wearing" as children of the King. God's designer clothing (compassion, kindness, humility, gentleness, and patience) never goes out of style and never wears out. Use this verse as a frequent reminder of what we are to wear in our daily interactions with each other. Encourage your kids when you see them "wearing" one of the qualities from the verse . . . letting them know how "good it looks on them."

—"Hey champ . . . here's your coat. It's going to be freezing out there today. And by the way . . . I noticed the coat of compassion you put on yesterday when your sister wasn't feeling well. It looked great on you! Remember that verse we learned? . . ."

Devo Five
· · · · · · · · · ·

"Do not be misled:
'Bad company corrupts good character.'"
1 Corinthians 15:33

You'll need:

Dirt, water, a pie tin, spoons (mud pie ingredients)

A blank index card and Bible for each family member

Activity:

As a family, read 1 Corinthians 15:33 and then underline it in your Bibles. Have each family member write the verse out on a blank index card.

Spend a few minutes talking about the verse. Explain that the word *corrupt* means "to destroy, pollute, stain, spoil, damage, infect." The word *character* means our "moral strength or reputation."

Have each family member wash their hands with soap and get them squeaky clean. Then head outside with the pie tin, water and spoons. Let the kids make their own mud pie creation. Your kids will love this. They may want to decorate the top with leaves and twigs, etc.

When they are all done creating their original mud pie, ask them to look at their recently washed hands. What do they look like? After playing in the dirt and water, their hands are now a muddy mess. Now ask them to look at their mud pie. Did any of their sqeaky clean hands "rub off" on the dirt? Do they see any "clean hand" in the mud? Of course not. Because when we play in the dirt our hands get muddy . . . the mud doesn't get "handy."

Share:

Our memory verse tells us not to be misled—bad company corrupts good character. None of us were surprised that playing in the mud was going to make our clean hands a muddy mess. We know that the mud will rub off on our hands, but our hands won't rub off on the mud.

Think of bad company (bad friendships) as a big mud pie. You can't hang around in the mud and not become a muddy mess. If we aren't careful who we hang around, our good character—behavior, attitudes, and reputation—can get really messed up and dirty. The Lord warns up to stay away from friends that will muddy up our good character.

On the other hand, it's important that we be a good influence to our friends as well. We don't want to be a "muddy" influence on others, do we?

God wants us to be really careful who we hang around so we can keep our hands and lives clean for him.

Seeing the Word Come to Life:

We can "see" this verse anytime our kids get dirty from playing outside. Talk about this verse when you are stain treating clothes they've been wearing when playing outside. Show them how the grass and dirt messed up their clothes, but they left nothing of themselves on the grass and dirt. Think of laundry detergent or spot remover as a great symbol for the influence of bad company—the wrong friends can leave a stain on us that isn't easy to get out.

—"Oh my goodness . . . just look at you! By the look of those dirty pants I can tell you must have had a great time on the playground at school today. That dirt sure made its mark on you. Hey, remember that verse we learned? . . ."

Learning Longer Passages

Some of the richest treasures in Scripture memory come from learning longer passages, even whole chapters of God's Word. For many of us, the thought of memorizing a bigger chunk of Scripture seems overwhelming. But it doesn't have to be.

Perhaps you've heard the riddle, "How do you eat an elephant?" The answer—"One bite at a time."

That's how it is with memorizing longer passages. Learning one line at a time enables us to "consume" larger portions of God's Word in manageable "bite-sized" pieces.

Formatting verses

It is much easier to learn a longer passage once it has been put into a simple line-by-line format. Here's an example of John 14:1–3 as it is found in the Bible:

> [1]"Do not let your hearts be troubled. Trust in God; trust also in me. [2]In my Father's house are many rooms; if it were not so, I would have told you. I am going there to prepare a place for you. [3]And if I go and prepare a place for you, I will come back and take you to be with me that you also may be where I am."

Now let's look at an example of the same passage in an easy-to-learn, line-by-line format:

1. "Do not let your hearts be troubled.
   Trust in God;
   trust also in me.
2. In my Father's house are many rooms;
   if it were not so, I would have told you.
   I am going there to *prepare a place for you.*
3. And if I go and *prepare a place for you,*
   I will come back and take you to be with me
   that you also may be where I am."

With a few helpful hints, your family can successfully learn longer passages of Scripture. Consider these useful ideas:

Write or type out the passage in large, easy-to-read font.

Format the verse line by line.

Underline, bold, and/or italicize key words.

Color-code the passage by verse or section, using one color per verse or section. (Be sure to use an ink color that is dark enough to read without difficulty.)

Print the passage out on computer paper with a design that is easily associated with the passage. (These designer computer papers are inexpensive and available at local copy or print stores)
For example:
"Cloud" design paper for 1 Thessalonians 4:13–18 which

refers to the Second Coming of the Lord Jesus.

"Grassy" design paper for Psalm 23, "The Lord is my Shepherd . . ."

"Scroll" design paper works well for the 10 Commandments or other Old Testament passages.

Place the printed page in a protective 3-ring plastic sleeve. (available at office supply or scrapbook stores) Give one copy to each family member and keep a copy in the car for drive time.

Buy a 3-ring binder for each member of your family. Once you've memorized the passage, put the copy of the printed passage in the binder for easy organization and review.

• • • • • • •

Don't quit—Keep going!
Stay committed to growing a well-versed family!

Verses for Life

In the beginning God created the heavens and the earth.

Genesis 1:1

The grass withers and the flowers fall, but the word of our God stands forever.

Isaiah 40:8

Your love, O Lord, reaches to the heavens, your faithfulness to the skies.

Psalm 36:5

Children, obey your parents in the Lord, for this is right.

Ephesians 6:1

When I am afraid, I will trust in you.

Psalm 56:3

Do not be misled: "Bad company corrupts good character."

1 Corinthians 15:33

Psalm 36:5

Isaiah 40:8

Genesis 1:1

1 Corinthians 15:33

Psalm 56:3

Ephesians 6:1

Verses for Life

Delight yourself in the Lord
and he will give you the
desires of your heart.

Psalm 37:4

Therefore, if anyone is in Christ,
he is a new creation;
the old has gone,
the new has come!

2 Corinthians 5:17

Love the Lord your God
with all your heart
and with all your soul
and with all your mind
and with all your strength.

Mark 12:30

But the fruit of the Spirit is love,
joy, peace, patience, kindness,
goodness, faithfulness,
gentleness and self-control.

Galatians 5:22–23

For nothing is impossible
with God.

Luke 1:37

Your word is a lamp to my feet
and a light for my path.

Psalm 119:105

Psalm 37:4

Mark 12:30

Luke 1:37

2 Corinthians 5:17

Galatians 5:22–23

Psalm 119:105

Verses for Life

Have I not commanded you?
Be strong and courageous.
Do not be terrified; do not be
discouraged, for the Lord your God
will be with you wherever you go.

Joshua 1:9

In the same way, let your light
shine before men, that they
may see your good deeds and
praise your Father in heaven.

Matthew 5:16

As far as the east is from the west,
so far has he removed our
transgressions from us.

Psalm 103:12

Whoever can be trusted with
very little can also be trusted
with much, and whoever is
dishonest with very little
will also be dishonest with much.

Luke 16:10

This is love:
not that we loved God,
but that he loved us
and sent his Son
as an atoning sacrifice for our sins.

1 John 4:10

Bear with each other and forgive
whatever grievance you may
have against one another.
Forgive as the Lord forgave you.

Colossians 3:13

Psalm 103:12

Matthew 5:16

Joshua 1:9

Colossians 3:13

1 John 4:10

Luke 16:10

Verses for Life

Cast all your anxiety on him because he cares for you.

1 Peter 5:7

The Lord does not look at the things man looks at. Man looks at the outward appearance, but the Lord looks at the heart.

1 Samuel 16:7

Therefore, as God's chosen people, holy and dearly loved, clothe yourselves with compassion, kindness, humility, gentleness and patience.

Colossians 3:12

I praise you because I am fearfully and wonderfully made; your works are wonderful, I know that full well.

Psalm 139:14

If we confess our sins, he is faithful and just and will forgive us our sins and purify us from all unrighteousness.

1 John 1:9

This is love for God: to obey his commands. And his commands are not burdensome.

1 John 5:3

Colossians 3:12

1 Samuel 16:7

1 Peter 5:7

1 John 5:3

1 John 1:9

Psalm 139:14

Verses for Life

I have hidden your word
in my heart that I might
not sin against you.

Psalm 119:11

All Scripture is God-breathed
and is useful for teaching,
rebuking, correcting and
training in righteousness.

2 Timothy 3:16

Do not be overcome by evil,
but overcome evil with good.

Romans 12:21

And without faith it is impossible
to please God, because anyone
who comes to him must
believe that he exists
and that he rewards those who
earnestly seek him.

Hebrews 11:6

And my God will meet all your
needs according to his glorious
riches in Christ Jesus.

Philippians 4:19

Do to others
as you would have them do to you.

Luke 6:31

Psalm 119:11

Romans 12:21

Philippians 4:19

2 Timothy 3:16

Hebrews 11:6

Luke 6:31

Verses for Life

I can do everything through him who gives me strength.

Philippians 4:13

No temptation has seized you except what is common to man. And God is faithful; He will not let you be tempted beyond what you can bear. But when you are tempted, he will also provide a way out so that you can stand up under it.

1 Corinthians 10:13

Look to the Lord and his strength; seek his face always.

Psalm 105:4

My dear brothers, take note of this: Everyone should be quick to listen, slow to speak and slow to become angry, for man's anger does not bring about the righteous life that God desires.

James 1:19–20

For God did not give us a spirit of timidity, but a spirit of power, of love and of self-discipline.

2 Timothy 1:7

But our citizenship is in heaven. And we eagerly await a Savior from there, the Lord Jesus Christ, who, by the power that enables him to bring everything under his control, will transform our lowly bodies so that they will be like his glorious body.

Philippians 3:20–21

2 Timothy 1:7

Psalm 105:4

Philippians 4:13

Philippians 3:20-21

James 1:19-20

1 Corinthians 10:13

Verses for Life

Don't let anyone look down on you because you are young, but set an example for the believers in speech, in life, in love, in faith and in purity.

1 Timothy 4:12

Every good and perfect gift is from above, coming down from the Father of heavenly lights, who does not change like shifting shadows.

James 1:17

But as for you, be strong and do not give up, for your work will be rewarded.

2 Chronicles 15:7

For even the Son of Man did not come to be served, but to serve, and to give his life as a ransom for many."

Mark 10:45

And as for you, brothers, never tire of doing what is right.

2 Thessalonians 3:13

Whatever you do, work at it with all your heart, as working for the Lord, not for men.

Colossians 3:23

1 Timothy 4:12

2 Chronicles 15:7

2 Thessalonians 3:13

James 1:17

Mark 10:45

Colossians 3:23

Verses for Life

And we know that in all things
God works for the good of those
who love him, who have been
called according to his purpose.

Romans 8:28

Neither height nor depth,
nor anything else in all creation,
will be able to separate us
from the love of God
that is in Christ Jesus our Lord.

Romans 8:39

Romans 8:28

Romans 8:39

The Wisdom of Proverbs

Trust in the Lord with all your heart
and lean not on your own
understanding;
In all your ways acknowledge him,
and he will make your
paths straight.

Proverbs 3:5–6

Even a child is known by his
actions, by whether his conduct
is pure and right.

Proverbs 20:11

A gentle answer turns away wrath,
but a harsh word stirs
up anger.

Proverbs 15:1

Above all else,
guard your heart,
for it is the wellspring of life.

Proverbs 4:23

The Lord detests lying lips,
but he delights in men who
are truthful.

Proverbs 12:22

The name of the Lord is a
strong tower;
the righteous run to it and
are safe.

Proverbs 18:10

Proverbs 15:1

Proverbs 20:11

Proverbs 3:5-6

Proverbs 18:10

Proverbs 12:22

Proverbs 4:23

The Wisdom of Proverbs

Pleasant words are a honeycomb,
sweet to the soul
and healing to the bones.

Proverbs 16:24

A fool shows his annoyance at
once, but a prudent man overlooks
an insult.

Proverbs 12:16

He who walks with the wise grows
wise, but a companion of fools
suffers harm.

Proverbs 13:20

The eyes of the Lord are everywhere, keeping watch on the wicked
and the good.

Proverbs 15:3

A heart at peace gives life to the
body, but envy rots the bones.

Proverbs 14:30

Pride goes before destruction,
a haughty spirit before a fall.

Proverbs 16:18

Proverbs 13:20

Proverbs 12:16

Proverbs 16:24

Proverbs 16:18

Proverbs 14:30

Proverbs 15:3

The Wisdom of Proverbs

To do what is right and just
is more acceptable to the Lord
than sacrifice.

Proverbs 21:3

The fear of the Lord
is the beginning of knowledge,
but fools despise wisdom
and discipline.

Proverbs 1:7

The highway of the upright
avoids evil;
he who guards his way guards
his life.

Proverbs 16:17

Honor the Lord with your wealth,
with the firstfruits of all your crops.

Proverbs 3:9

He who conceals his sins does not
prosper, but whoever
confesses and renounces them
finds mercy.

Proverbs 28:13

Blessed is the man
who always fears the Lord,
but he who hardens his heart
falls into trouble.

Proverbs 28:14

Proverbs 21:3

Proverbs 16:17

Proverbs 28:13

Proverbs 1:7

Proverbs 3:9

Proverbs 28:14

The Wisdom of Proverbs

Like a gold ring in a pig's snout
is a beautiful woman who shows
no discretion.

Proverbs 11:22

Reckless words pierce like a sword,
but the tongue of the wise
brings healing.

Proverbs 12:18

Gold there is, and rubies in
abundance, but lips that speak
knowledge are a rare jewel.

Proverbs 20:15

My son,
if sinners entice you,
do not give in to them.

Proverbs 1:10

A friend loves at all times,
and a brother is born for adversity.

Proverbs 17:17

A generous man will prosper;
he who refreshes others will himself
be refreshed.

Proverbs 11:25

Proverbs 21:3

Proverbs 16:17

Proverbs 28:13

Proverbs 1:7

Proverbs 3:9

Proverbs 28:14

The Wisdom of Proverbs

As iron sharpens iron,
so one man sharpens another.

Proverbs 27:17

All hard work brings a profit, but
mere talk leads only to poverty.

Proverbs 14:23

Commit to the Lord whatever you
do, and your plans
will succeed.

Proverbs 16:3

Proverbs 27:17

Proverbs 14:23

Proverbs 16:3

Verses for Faith and Salvation The Six "For's"

For all have sinned and fall short of the glory of God.

Romans 3:23

For God so loved the world that he gave his one and only Son, that whoever believes in him shall not perish but have eternal life.

John 3:16

For what I received I passed on to you as of first importance: that Christ died for our sins according to the Scriptures, that he was buried, that he was raised on the third day according to the Scriptures.

1 Corinthians 15:3-4

For the wages of sin is death, but the gift of God is eternal life in Jesus Christ our Lord.

Romans 6:23

For there is one God and one mediator between God and men, the man Christ Jesus.

1 Timothy 2:5

For it is by grace you have been saved, through faith—and this not from yourselves, it is the gift of God—not by works, so that no one can boast.

Ephesians 2:8-9

1 Corinthians 15:3-4

John 3:16

Romans 3:23

Ephesians 2:8-9

1 Timothy 2:5

Romans 6:23

The Seven "I Am"s of Jesus

"I am the bread of life.
He who comes to me will never
go hungry, and he who believes
in me will never be thirsty."

John 6:35

"I am the light of the world.
Whoever follows me will
never walk in darkness,
but will have the light of life."

John 8:12

"I am the gate;
whoever enters through me
will be saved."

John 10:9

"I am the good shepherd.
The good shepherd
lays down his life for the sheep."

John 10:11

"I am the resurrection and the life.
He who believes in me will
live, even though he dies; and
whoever lives and believes
in me will never die."

John 11:25–26

"I am the way and the truth
and the life.
No one comes to the Father
except through me."

John 14:6

John 11:25-26

John 10:9

John 6:35

John 14:6

John 10:11

John 8:12

The Seven "I Am"s of Jesus

"I am the vine; you are the branches. If a man remains in me and I in him, he will bear much fruit; apart from me you can do nothing."

John 15:5

John 15:5

Suggested Longer Passages

1. Psalm 1 (Two Men, Two Ways, Two Destinies)
2. Psalm 100 (A Psalm of Praise)
3. Psalm 23 (The Faithful Shepherd)
4. 1 Corinthians 13 (Love)
5. Philippians 2:1–16 (Christ—Our Example)
6. Matthew 6:9–13 (Prayer)
7. 1 Thessalonians 4:13–18 (The Second Coming of Christ)
8. Ephesians 6:10–18 (The Armor of God)
9. Colossians 2:6–10 (Life in Christ)
10. Luke 2:1–20 (The Birth of Jesus)
11. John 14:1–4 (The Promise of Heaven)
12. Hebrews 12:1–3 (Fixing our Eyes on Jesus)

Endnotes

1   Deuteronomy 6:7
2   Psalm 119:111
3   May, Steve. *The Story File*. Hendrickson Publishers. 2000. pg. 170.
4   *Preaching Today*, Tape 172
5   White, Joe. *What Kids Wish Parents Knew About Parenting*. Questar Publishers, Inc. 1988. pg. 55.
6   Proverbs 4:23
7   Susan Mitchell, *The Official Guide to the Generations* (Washington, D.C.: U.S. Department of Education, Census Bureau, 1995), 12.
8   Knight-Ridder Tribune News, 1989
9   Colossians 4:10
10   Proverbs 4:4
11   Proverbs 4:5
12   Proverbs 7:3
13   Proverbs 22:18
14   Matthew 4:1–11
15   *Growing Strong in the Seasons of Life*, Multinomah Press, 1983, pg.53. (As written with italics)
16   White, Joe. *Faith Training*. Tyndale House Publishers. 1994. pg 58
17   White, Joe. *Faith Training*. Tyndale House Publishers. 1994. pg 58
18   *The 7 Habits of Highly Effective Families*, Stephen R. Covey, 1995, Tape 4

19   Webster's New World Dictionary and Thesaurus, Mac Millan, 1996.

20   Deuteronomy 11:18

21   Webster's New World Dictionary and Thesaurus, Mac Millan, 1996.

22   John 14:21

23   Matthew 15:8

24   Pulpit Helps, July 1999, p. 6.

25   Children and Family Ministry Infosource Newsletter, CFM Infosource, Fall 2000, Portland, Oregon

26   James S. Hewett, *Illustrations Unlimited* (Wheaton: Tyndale House Publishers., 1988)

27   Dr. Joe White, *Faith Training*, Wheaton: Tyndale House Publishers, 1994, pg 54.

28   Proverbs 16:21

29   Rick Kirkman and Jerry Scott, *Baby Blues*, King Features Syndicate, Inc.

30   Hebrews 3:13

31   Steve May, *The Story File* (Hendrickson Publishers, 2000)

32   James 1:5

33   Romans 15:13

34   Psalm 51:12

35   I Corinthians 3:6,8

36   John Woodbridge, *Great Leaders of the Christian Church.*

37   I John 4:19

38   Steve May, *The Story File*, Hendrickson Publishers, 2000

39   Proclaim, July-Sept. 1991, pg 29

40   Proverbs 1:20–21

41   *Too Old Too Soon*, Doug Fields, 1991

42   "A Lost Eloquence," Carol Muske-Dukes, New York Times, December 29, 2002,

43   *Memorize the Word*, Moody Press, 1970, pg 15.

44   *Memorize the Word*, Moody Press, 1970, pg 50.

45   Transcript of NBC "Dateline" program, December 13, 1999. Burrelles's Information Services.

46   Matthew 4:19

47   John 6:35

48   John 8:12, John 10:9, John 10:11, John 15:1

49   Matthew 5:26, 28

50   Matthew 7:15 and Matthew 5:13

51   "Making Mneumories," Caralee J. Adams, *Better Homes and Gardens*, September 2000.

52   Grant, George. *Carry a Big Stick*. Cumberland House Publishing, Inc. 1996. pg. 110.

53   Philippians 2:14

54   Transcript of NBC "Dateline" program, December 13, 1999. Burrelles's Information Services.

55   Crossroads, V01.1, No. 4, p. 23

56   Charles R. Swindoll, *The Strong Family. Living on the Ragged Edge.*

57   David Hubbard, *Beyond Futility*

58   Matthew 16:13–16, Mark 6:29, Luke 9:20

59   Billy Graham, *'Til Armageddon* (Minneapolis: World Wide, 1981), 9.

60   Howard and Phyllis Rutledge and Mel and Lyla White, *In the Presence of Mine Enemies* (Old Tappan, NJ: Flemming H. Revell Co., 1973).

61   Ruth Bell Graham, *It's My Turn* (Old Tappan, NJ: Flemming H. Revell Co., 1982), 172

62   Gloria Gaither, Shirley Dobson. *Let's Hide the Word.* Word Publishing. 1994. pg 143.

63   *Vines Expository Dictionary of New Testament Words*, MacDonald Publishing Company. Pg 736.

About the Author

Warm, witty, and wise. These are a few of the adjectives used to describe Caroline Boykin. Blessed with a godly heritage, she was taught to memorize God's Word from early childhood. Today, Caroline is passionate about Scripture Memory—and the next generation! As a mom, she has created fun, easy and effective ways to successfully plant the Word in the heart of her home. She is a dynamic speaker who inspires and equips parents to raise great kids of faith through Scripture memory. Caroline has led numerous Bible Studies, taught Sunday school to preschoolers, and has served as a mentor in Women's' ministry. She holds a Bachelors Degree in Nutrition, and had a career in the pharmaceutical industry for over 10 years. She has worked as an elementary school teaching assistant, and currently serves on the Board of Trustees at a Christian Academy in Dallas. Caroline and her husband, Lindsay, have two daughters and live in Plano, Texas.

To contact Caroline, visit www.wellversedfamily.com.

Endorsements

"To memorize God's word is one thing, to memorize and apply is another. Caroline helps equip moms and dads with the most powerful parenting resource of all – God's Word!! Through strong parental involvement and modeling – of which I am a big fan, Scripture moves from head knowledge to heart transformation. This "spiritual home schooling" resource is a must for every family."

—Jim Weidmann
Executive Director
Heritage Builders/Focus on the Family
"The Family Night Guy"

• • • • • • •

"What a delight it is to recommend this book to you. I cannot think of a greater gift to give our children than the Word of God tucked up in their hearts. In an ever changing world we can know that God loves us, that He is in control and He has given us His word as a rock to build our lives upon. You will love this book!"

—Sheila Walsh
Women of Faith speaker
Author of God Has a Dream for Your Life

"This is a must read for every parent! It's highly motivational, intensely practical – and most of all truly biblical! My friend, Caroline, writes from her parental experience – and from her heart."

—Dr. Gene A. Getz
Pastor Emeritus, Fellowship Bible Church North
President, Center for Church Renewal

• • • • • • •

"Caroline Boykin is a gifted writer who clearly and winsomely convinces you of the value of memorizing Scripture. Then she gives you an easy to implement plan to hide God's Word in your heart. I would have loved to have had Caroline as my mother! I highly recommend The Well-Versed Family to anyone who genuinely desires to develop an intimate relationship with the Lord and impact those around them."

—Edwina Patterson
Author, Speaker, Founder of Redeeming the Time Ministry

• • • • • • •

"What parent doesn't fear for his or her children, living as we do in a society where so many of the games they are invited to play, are lethal? In this book, Caroline Boykin shows us how we, as parents, can provide a powerful antidote that will be with our children to protect them for the rest of their lives. What's more, parenting, as this book describes it, is not just about helping our children grow. It is also an unparalleled opportunity to deepen our own intimacy with God as we disciple our children."

—Jim Petersen
Former International Vice President of the Navigators,
Missionary, and Author

Suggested Longer Passages

1. Psalm 1 (Two Men, Two Ways, Two Destinies)
2. Psalm 100 (A Psalm of Praise)
3. Psalm 23 (The Faithful Shepherd)
4. 1 Corinthians 13 (Love)
5. Philippians 2:1–16 (Christ—Our Example)
6. Matthew 6:9–13 (Prayer)
7. 1 Thessalonians 4:13–18 (The Second Coming of Christ)
8. Ephesians 6:10–18 (The Armor of God)
9. Colossians 2:6–10 (Life in Christ)
10. Luke 2:1–20 (The Birth of Jesus)
11. John 14:1–4 (The Promise of Heaven)
12. Hebrews 12:1–3 (Fixing our Eyes on Jesus)

Endnotes

1   Deuteronomy 6:7

2   Psalm 119:111

3   May, Steve. *The Story File*. Hendrickson Publishers. 2000. pg. 170.

4   *Preaching Today*, Tape 172

5   White, Joe. *What Kids Wish Parents Knew About Parenting*. Questar Publishers, Inc. 1988. pg. 55.

6   Proverbs 4:23

7   Susan Mitchell, *The Official Guide to the Generations* (Washington, D.C.: U.S. Department of Education, Census Bureau, 1995), 12.

8   Knight-Ridder Tribune News, 1989

9   Colossians 4:10

10 Proverbs 4:4

11 Proverbs 4:5

12 Proverbs 7:3

13 Proverbs 22:18

14 Matthew 4:1–11

15 *Growing Strong in the Seasons of Life*, Multinomah Press, 1983, pg.53. (As written with italics)

16 White, Joe. *Faith Training*. Tyndale House Publishers. 1994. pg 58

17 White, Joe. *Faith Training*. Tyndale House Publishers. 1994. pg 58

18 *The 7 Habits of Highly Effective Families*, Stephen R. Covey, 1995, Tape 4

19   Webster's New World Dictionary and Thesaurus, Mac Millan, 1996.

20   Deuteronomy 11:18

21   Webster's New World Dictionary and Thesaurus, Mac Millan, 1996.

22   John 14:21

23   Matthew 15:8

24   Pulpit Helps, July 1999, p. 6.

25   Children and Family Ministry Infosource Newsletter, CFM Infosource, Fall 2000, Portland, Oregon

26   James S. Hewett, *Illustrations Unlimited* (Wheaton: Tyndale House Publishers., 1988)

27   Dr. Joe White, *Faith Training*, Wheaton: Tyndale House Publishers, 1994, pg 54.

28   Proverbs 16:21

29   Rick Kirkman and Jerry Scott, *Baby Blues*, King Features Syndicate, Inc.

30   Hebrews 3:13

31   Steve May, *The Story File* (Hendrickson Publishers, 2000)

32   James 1:5

33   Romans 15:13

34   Psalm 51:12

35   I Corinthians 3:6,8

36   John Woodbridge, *Great Leaders of the Christian Church.*

37   I John 4:19

38   Steve May, *The Story File*, Hendrickson Publishers, 2000

39   Proclaim, July-Sept. 1991, pg 29

40   Proverbs 1:20–21

41   *Too Old Too Soon*, Doug Fields, 1991

42   "A Lost Eloquence," Carol Muske-Dukes, New York Times, December 29, 2002,

43   *Memorize the Word*, Moody Press, 1970, pg 15.

44   *Memorize the Word*, Moody Press, 1970, pg 50.

45   Transcript of NBC "Dateline" program, December 13, 1999. Burrelles's Information Services.

46   Matthew 4:19

47   John 6:35

48   John 8:12, John 10:9, John 10:11, John 15:1

49   Matthew 5:26, 28

50   Matthew 7:15 and Matthew 5:13

51   "Making Mneumories," Caralee J. Adams, *Better Homes and Gardens*, September 2000.

52   Grant, George. *Carry a Big Stick*. Cumberland House Publishing, Inc. 1996. pg. 110.

53   Philippians 2:14

54   Transcript of NBC "Dateline" program, December 13, 1999. Burrelles's Information Services.

55   Crossroads, V01.1, No. 4, p. 23

56   Charles R. Swindoll, *The Strong Family. Living on the Ragged Edge.*

57   David Hubbard, *Beyond Futility*

58   Matthew 16:13–16, Mark 6:29, Luke 9:20

59   Billy Graham, *'Til Armageddon* (Minneapolis: World Wide, 1981), 9.

60   Howard and Phyllis Rutledge and Mel and Lyla White, *In the Presence of Mine Enemies* (Old Tappan, NJ: Flemming H. Revell Co., 1973).

61   Ruth Bell Graham, *It's My Turn* (Old Tappan, NJ: Flemming H. Revell Co., 1982), 172

62   Gloria Gaither, Shirley Dobson. *Let's Hide the Word.* Word Publishing. 1994. pg 143.

63   *Vines Expository Dictionary of New Testament Words*, MacDonald Publishing Company. Pg 736.

About the Author

Warm, witty, and wise. These are a few of the adjectives used to describe Caroline Boykin. Blessed with a godly heritage, she was taught to memorize God's Word from early childhood. Today, Caroline is passionate about Scripture Memory—and the next generation! As a mom, she has created fun, easy and effective ways to successfully plant the Word in the heart of her home. She is a dynamic speaker who inspires and equips parents to raise great kids of faith through Scripture memory. Caroline has led numerous Bible Studies, taught Sunday school to preschoolers, and has served as a mentor in Women's' ministry. She holds a Bachelors Degree in Nutrition, and had a career in the pharmaceutical industry for over 10 years. She has worked as an elementary school teaching assistant, and currently serves on the Board of Trustees at a Christian Academy in Dallas. Caroline and her husband, Lindsay, have two daughters and live in Plano, Texas.

To contact Caroline, visit www.wellversedfamily.com.

Endorsements

"To memorize God's word is one thing, to memorize and apply is another. Caroline helps equip moms and dads with the most powerful parenting resource of all – God's Word!! Through strong parental involvement and modeling – of which I am a big fan, Scripture moves from head knowledge to heart transformation. This "spiritual home schooling" resource is a must for every family."

—Jim Weidmann
Executive Director
Heritage Builders/Focus on the Family
"The Family Night Guy"

• • • • • • •

"What a delight it is to recommend this book to you. I cannot think of a greater gift to give our children than the Word of God tucked up in their hearts. In an ever changing world we can know that God loves us, that He is in control and He has given us His word as a rock to build our lives upon. You will love this book!"

—Sheila Walsh
Women of Faith speaker
Author of God Has a Dream for Your Life

"This is a must read for every parent! It's highly motivational, intensely practical – and most of all truly biblical! My friend, Caroline, writes from her parental experience – and from her heart."

—Dr. Gene A. Getz
Pastor Emeritus, Fellowship Bible Church North
President, Center for Church Renewal

. . . .

"Caroline Boykin is a gifted writer who clearly and winsomely convinces you of the value of memorizing Scripture. Then she gives you an easy to implement plan to hide God's Word in your heart. I would have loved to have had Caroline as my mother! I highly recommend The Well-Versed Family to anyone who genuinely desires to develop an intimate relationship with the Lord and impact those around them."

—Edwina Patterson
Author, Speaker, Founder of Redeeming the Time Ministry

. . . .

"What parent doesn't fear for his or her children, living as we do in a society where so many of the games they are invited to play, are lethal? In this book, Caroline Boykin shows us how we, as parents, can provide a powerful antidote that will be with our children to protect them for the rest of their lives. What's more, parenting, as this book describes it, is not just about helping our children grow. It is also an unparalleled opportunity to deepen our own intimacy with God as we disciple our children."

—Jim Petersen
Former International Vice President of the Navigators,
Missionary, and Author